The MUSIC of
WHAT HAPPENS

POEMS THAT TELL STORIES

A Richard Jackson Book

The MUSIC of WHAT HAPPENS

POEMS THAT TELL STORIES

Selected by Paul B. Janeczko

ORCHARD BOOKS   NEW YORK

A division of Franklin Watts, Inc.

Orchard Books,
387 Park Avenue South, New York, New York 10016

Orchard Books Canada,
20 Torbay Road, Markham, Ontario 23P 1G6

Orchard Books is a division of Franklin Watts, Inc.

Manufactured in the United States of America
Book design by Mina Greenstein
The text of this book is set in 12 pt. Caslon 540
2 4 6 8 10 9 7 5 3 1

Library of Congress Cataloging-in-Publication Data
The Music of what happens: poems that tell stories: a selection / by
Paul B. Janeczko. Includes index. Summary: A collection of bitter-
sweet, thought-provoking poems by a variety of modern authors.
ISBN 0-531-05757-7 ISBN 0-531-08357-8 (lib. bdg.).
1. Narrative poetry, American. 2. Children's poetry, American.
[1. Narrative poetry. 2. American poetry—Collections.]
I. Janeczko, Paul B.
PS593.N2M87 1988 811'.03'08—dc19 87-30791 CIP AC

This collection is dedicated to
MELANIE MAY
and
NORMA RICHMAN VOGEL

———

Thank you, ladies,
for your friendship,
a story that began in another life
for all of us.

The Finest Music

Once, as they rested on a chase, a debate arose among the Fianna-Finn as to what was the finest music in the world.

"Tell us that," said Fionn, turning to Oisin.

"The cuckoo calling from the tree that is highest in the hedge," cried his merry son.

"A good sound," said Fionn. "And you, Oscar," he asked, "what is to your mind the finest of music?"

"The top of music is the ring of a spear on a shield," cried the stout lad.

"It is a good sound," said Fionn.

And the other champions told their delight: the belling of a stag across water, the baying of a tuneful pack heard in the distance, the song of a lark, the laughter of a gleeful girl, or the whisper of a moved one.

"They are good sounds all," said Fionn.

"Tell us, chief," one ventured, "what do you think?"

"The music of what happens," said great Fionn, "that is the finest music in the world."

—JAMES STEPHENS,
Irish Fairy Stories

CONTENTS

The MUSIC of WHAT HAPPENS

POEMS THAT TELL STORIES

The Purpose of Poetry

This old man grazed thirty head of cattle
in a valley just north of the covered bridge
on the Mississinewa, where the reservoir
stands today. Had a black border collie
and a half-breed sheep dog with one eye.
The dogs took the cows to pasture each morning
and brought them home again at night
and herded them into the barn. The old man
would slip a wooden bar across both doors.
One dog slept on the front porch, one on the back.

He was waiting there one evening
listening to the animals coming home
when a man from the courthouse stopped
to tell him how the new reservoir
was going to flood all his property.
They both knew he was too far up in years
to farm anywhere else. He had a daughter
who lived in Florida, in a trailer park.
He should sell now and go stay with her.
The man helped bar the doors before he left.

He had only known dirt under his fingernails
and trips to town on Saturday mornings
since he was a boy. Always he had been around
cattle, and trees, and land near the river.
Evenings by the barn he could hear the dogs
talking to each other as they brought in
the herd; and the cows answering them.
It was the clearest thing he knew. That night
he shot both dogs and then himself.
The purpose of poetry is to tell us about life.

Finding a Lucky Number

To a nephew

When I was like you I crossed a street
To a store, and from the store
Up an alley, as I rolled chocolate
In my mouth and looked around
With my face. The day was blue
Between trees, even without wind,
And the fences were steaming
And a dog was staring into a paint bucket
And a Mexicano was raking
Spilled garbage into a box,
A raffle of eggshells and orange peels.
He nodded his head and I nodded mine
And rolled chocolate all the way
To the courthouse, where I sat
In the park, with a leaf falling
For every person who passed—
Three leaves and three daughters
With bags in their hands.
I followed them under trees,
The leaves rocking out of reach
Like those skirts I would love
From a distance. I lost them
When I bent down to tie my shoes
And begged a squirrel to eat grass.
Looking up, a dog on the run,
A grandma with a cart,
And Italians clicking dominoes
At a picnic table—men
Of the old world, in suits big enough
For Europe. I approached
Them like a squirrel, a tree
At a time, and when I was close

Enough to tell the hour from their wrists,
One laughed with hands in his hair
And turned to ask my age.
"Twelve," I said, and he knocked
My head softly with a knuckle:
"Lucky number, Sonny." He bared
His teeth, yellow and crooked
As dominoes, and tapped the front ones
With a finger. "I got twelve—see."
He opened wide until his eyes were lost
In the pouches of fat cheeks,
And I, not knowing what to do, looked in.

In the Spring

The football coach coached tennis in the spring.
A nincompoop with a whistle still round his neck,
who made us scream our ritualized replies to
Who's going to win! Who! I can't hear you!
Always that, before stepping on the court to play.

The woods hadn't yet receded from around our town,
and he knew farm boys had no use in later life
for a game involving love and sissy clothes.
He'd demonstrate a stroke once in a while
like a ninny swatting a hornet with an oar;

the game he showed us was a blasphemy, brash,
unmannered, dangerous and mean.
Bring him to the net, he'd say, and squash one
at his face; he'll give up when his eyes swell shut.
Manners are for cowards who only want to win
if they don't have to beat you.

Because of what he did each fall, we gave ourselves
to him every spring. The jonquils flourished
and the dogwoods bloomed and robins cracked awake
out through their shells and sang.
While Coach stomped across the court in spikes
to pass on the secrets of his dying sport.

The Flood

When I sat beside the river
Thinking of waves higher than buildings
Waves descending like barges down the smooth channel
I thought I dreamed.

But the water came high—
It filled the cellar
Covered grandmother's canned pears
And the quilts by the fireplace.

It rose above grandfather's portrait
Lapped at our feet on the second story.
We looked down the stairs.
Would the house hold?

Could we float on that Ark
Through the corn fields
Downtown past the first national bank
And Gluth's grocery store?

Logs and fence posts piled up by the house.
The pig flowed away, complaining.
Night was coming down,
The waters pushed at the foundations,
Our dog whined in the upstairs bedroom.

What could we do but sit there?
We made a raft of the bedstead
And a plank off the bedroom dresser.
We were ready to knock a hole in the wall
For launching. But the stream began to go down.

It went down to mud. The crops were gone,
The animals lost or dead. But we were alive.
The old house as good a ship as any.
Whenever I look at the river
I think of those waves and wonder.

Garbage

We hauled trash that summer, the three of us,
an old man, a hard young man, and a boy.
Morning by afternoon there were runs
to Whitzman Bros. scrap-metal yard
and to the dump on the outskirts of town.
The job was at Poole's Garage, cleaning out
a junkyard in the vacant lot next door.
The junk had to be sorted piece by piece,
salvage to one corner, the rest on the truck.
Mornings were for the metal, heavy stuff first.
We winched up motors, bulldogged transmissions
and rear axles, bowled rims from across the lot.
When the truck was half full of iron and steel,
we would top off the load with rusty tin—
doors, trunk-covers, stove-in hoods and fenders—
and haul it all away to the scales.

Afternoons we loaded up with garbage
the boss knew no one would ever pay to have:
rotten furniture, old bones, clutch-plates, rags.
Then smeared with dirt, three-deep in the cab,
we would drive it away to the water's edge
where roaring dozers butted the mounded trash
and rancid smoke coiled out of the debris.
After the first few times it was no surprise
to see him, a skinny black man in a peaked cap,
waiting to back us around to the edge
and watch with care our careless tossing-off.
He and his partners sifted each load
for something of value we had missed.
They set aside mud-filled bottles for refunds,
and wire that promised copper under the grease.
Broken boards they saved for winter fires
in windy shacks at the edge of the dump.

Their field-office crowned a hill of junk.
Two-by-fours and a door-frame held it up,
a rotten canvas canopy sagging above
old car seats and a disembowelled chair
where they dogged it when business was slow.
An ancient ice-box squatted to one side,
and from the door-frame hung a cowbell, clapperless.
Their look-out beat it with a tire-iron
when the police cruiser nosed into view.

The man sold bootleg liquor on the side.
On the day's last trip, and sometimes its first,
Grandad and Stu would buy a pint from him,
offer him a swallow and stand round his lean-to
drinking and yarning in the sunny stench.
They'd forget about Poole, his ninety cents an hour,
the black wind drifting low over the burning,
and I, just a kid then, would watch them,
listen carefully, begin to learn how it was
a man could live like this, if he had to.

Outhouse Blues

so much of my early
life was spent
suspended

above that black
and gargoyled
pit

hanging there
in the cold
ammonia draft

remembering the horror
stories of a cousin
who disappeared
forever

when he was
grabbed
from

below

Constipation

Stuck each summer at Bible camp
with the ten-year-old wits and prophets,
I would not be
the victim of hoots and whistles,
the object of chortles and leers.
I knew the body was holy.
So, chary of farts and gasses,
I squeezed it back all week,
and learned the proper responses:
He who smelt it, dealt it;
A skunk can't smell his own stink.

Until one night,
cramped up and desperate,
I sneaked out to the latrine,
and there saw Sally Harper,
immaculate in the moonlight,
angelic as a dream,
slide through the forbidden door
as the night filled with her
blats, toots, grunts, and raspberries.
And then I laughed myself silly,
and knew what a heaven was for.

What Saundra Said About Being Short

Back from camp that morning,
I stood on her porch waiting
with lanyards, leather bracelets,
ponytail holders, braided belts,
a wallet and a plaque, her name
hammered cockeyed or scorched
everywhere: Saundra, Saundra.
Saundra came to the door, a half
a foot taller than I'd left her
and with breasts and hair loose.
"You'll have to learn," she said,
"how to be quick and agile to still
make the teams, to scrap against
the quick mean short ones. You'll
always be in the front row of every
chorus, every class photo, hearing
me whisper from the back to the boys
who kept up with me. You'll have to
guard against bitterness and neck cramp,
and stay out of the deep end.
You'll have to learn to sit on dictionaries
and to crane up for a drink at the fountain.
Now that you know that we are over,
and that your growing is over too,
you'll have to find something new to hope for.
And this time, I suggest you make it
something within your grasp."

Elevation

Daddy made Evangeline and me
a little stool on which we milked
imaginary herds, and climbed to reach
the mysterious mesa of the bureau top
where the magazines and pamphlets were heaped.
Stepping up I saw the whole room new
and from the higher angle felt big,
finding the dust on the second shelf
of the china closet where
my grandpa kept his peppermints.
We used it as an elevator to get
above each other.
From higher up the whitehot veins
in the lightbulb were visible.
I could attain from its vantage the fishing tackle
Uncle James had left in the closet under the stairs,
and the little machine for rolling cigarettes
they shipped back from England
with Uncle Robert's trunk.
We raised ourselves on the pedestal
to command the window as snow fell
on William leading home the stock.
Best was mounting to browse
among the mantel junk: pens and letters,
needles, coins, toys forgotten weeks ago,
and often nuts, as well as medicine.
But Mama warned to stay away from the fireplace
and mantel; no climbing on the stool
around the hearth. Then after several days,
too curious about the trash around the clock,
I moved the compact podium onto the stone
and hoisted on its shaky footing
into the warmer zone where the keys
and calendar smelled like smoke.

She looked in from the kitchen
just in time to see me stretching there,
and rushed to pull me down and fling
the stand into the fire.
She had to hold me back as
flames soaked into the wood.
First the familiar legs and seat
got painted black and, sucked on by the light,
began to shrink. Bits of the foliage
climbed among the braces
as on a trellis.
I cried each time I looked
into the hell and saw the bones
pop and settle until nothing remained
of the beloved wood but petal ash,
while Mama rocked and the fireplace
cooled black and empty.

Driving Lesson

For Suzanne

Beside him in the old Ford pickup
that smelled of rope and grease and cattle feed,
sat my sister and I, ten and eight, big,
now our grandfather would teach us
that powerful secret, how to drive.
Horizon of high mountain peaks visible
above the blue hood, steering wheel huge
in our hands, pedals at our toe-tips,
we heard his sure voice urge us
Give it gas, give it gas. Over the roar
of the engine our hearts banged
like never before and banged on
furiously in the silence after
we bucked and stalled the truck.
How infinitely empty it then seemed—
windy flat rangeland of silver-green
gramma grass dotted with blooming cactus
and jagged outcrops of red rock, beginnings
of the Sangre de Cristos fifty miles off.
All Guadelupe County, New Mexico,
nothing to hit, and we could not
get the damn thing going. Nothing to hit
was no help. It was not the mechanics
of accelerator and clutch, muscle and bone,
but our sheer unruly spirits
that kept us small with the great desire
to move the world by us, earth and sky
and all the earth and sky contained.
And how hard it was when,
after our grandfather who was a god
said *Let it out slow, slow* time and again
until we did and were at long last rolling

over the earth, his happy little angels,
how hard it was to listen
not to our own thrilled inner voices
saying *Go, go,* but to his saying
the *Good, good* we loved but also
the *Keep it in the ruts* we hated to hear.
How hard to hold to it—
single red vein of a ranch road
running out straight across the mesa,
blood we were bound to follow—
when what we wanted with all our hearts
was to scatter everywhere, everywhere.

Gathering Strength

I looked over my shoulder
at the bedroom mirror and flexed my biceps.
I inspected my body and studied
the body of Charles Atlas in a comic book.

One time, Old Man Brunner winked
and told me how to build muscles—
every day carry a calf for ten minutes
until it's a cow and you're a gorilla.

In the barn, I bent over the calf,
put my left arm under the neck,
my right arm behind the back legs,
and stood up, the calf across my chest.

I marched in giant steps around the pen.
I dreamed about the people who would come
from all over to watch. The headlines
would say: Boy Carries Full-Grown Steer.

But through the dusty window, I looked
hard at the steers in the feedlot,
their blocky shoulders bumping for space
at the feedbunk. I set the calf down.

Cruel Boys

First day. Jackie and I walking in leaves
On our way to becoming 8th graders,
Pencils behind our ears, pee-chee folders
Already scribbled with football players
In dresses, track star in a drooped bra.
We're tough. I'm Mexican
And he's an unkillable Okie with three
Teeth in his pocket, sludge under
His nails from scratching oily pants.
No one's going to break us, not the dean
Or principal, not the cops
Who could arrive in pairs, walkie-talkies
To their mouths, warning:
"Dangerous. They have footballs."
We could bounce them off their heads
And reporters might show up
With shirt sleeves rolled up to their ears,
Asking our age, if we're Catholic.
But this never happens. We go to first
Period, math, then second period, geography,
And in third period, English, the woman
Teacher reads us Frost, something
About a tree, and to set things straight,
How each day will fall like a tree.
Jackie raises his hand, stands up,
And shouts, "You ain't nothing but a hound dog,"
As the spitballs begin to fly.

How I Learned English

It was in an empty lot
Ringed by elms and fir and honeysuckle.
Bill Corson was pitching in his buckskin jacket,
Chuck Keller, fat even as a boy, was on first,
His T-shirt riding up over his gut,
Ron O'Neill, Jim, Dennis, were talking it up
In the field, a blue sky above them
Tipped with cirrus.
                And there I was,
Just off the plane and plopped in the middle
Of Williamsport, Pa. and a neighborhood game,
Unnatural and without any moves,
My notions of baseball and America
Growing fuzzier each time I whiffed.

So it was not impossible that I,
Banished to the outfield and daydreaming
Of water, or a hotel in the mountains,
Would suddenly find myself in the path
Of a ball stung by Joe Barone.
I watched it closing in
Clean and untouched, transfixed
By its easy arc before it hit
My forehead with a thud.
                I fell back,
Dazed, clutching my brow,
Groaning, "Oh my shin, oh my shin,"
And everybody peeled away from me
And dropped from laughter, and there we were,
All of us writhing on the ground for one reason
Or another.
             Someone said "shin" again,
There was a wild stamping of hands on the ground,

A kicking of feet, and the fit
Of laughter overtook me too,
And that was important, as important
As Joe Barone asking me how I was
Through his tears, picking me up
And dusting me off with hands like swatters,
And though my head felt heavy,
I played on till dusk
Missing flies and pop-ups and grounders
And calling out in desperation things like
"Yours" and "take it," but doing all right,
Tugging at my cap in just the right way,
Crouching low, my feet set,
"Hum baby" sweetly on my lips.

Ophelia

Mr. G., my instructor, with wild eyes
And feet like a pigeon's, stands
In the shadows of the high school stage
Directing my speech with his hand
In his hair. I'm his
Ophelia this year, naming the fistful
Of herbs that isn't there,
Trying to imagine my brief life closing
In this lunacy.
                Tomorrow, says Mr. G.,
You will fall in the river, free
Of Hamlet's intelligent disdain. Enunciate!
O how the wheel becomes it!
You must see the fennel and the columbines.

It's after school, the janitor's cart
Squeaks down the hall, then his soft wide
Broom sweeps sawdust backstage.
Mr. G. comes closer, I am sixteen, he loves me
                        a little,
He looks at me with infinite sorrow
Then straightens his glasses.

In a few years he's out of there, selling
Insurance. I can still do
That Ophelia he'd know anywhere,
Stumbling, stuttering, never too clear.

The Kiss

"Come into the hall with me, George,"
said beautiful Miss Doyle, my French teacher,
whom I loved.
"I want to talk with you about your work.
You're so talented in the language, George,"
she said, closing the classroom door,
"and your accent is so genuine,
I wonder why you don't work more
and get the high grades you really deserve."
She leaned toward me kindly
and took my hands in hers.
In this dream of a fourteen-year old
I was trembling with joy
and the everlasting shyness of my life.
Then she hugged me and kissed me on the lips
with a kiss that was all confection
and fragrance and love,
sweetest of my life, asleep or awake,
a dream within a dream
that went on and on
as we rose through the roof
up to the white clouds
above John Adams High School
and sailed away
to the clop-clop of the milkman's horse.

The Sacred

After the teacher asked if anyone had
   a sacred place
and the students fidgeted and shrunk

in their chairs, the most serious of them all
   said it was his car,
being in it alone, his tape deck playing

things he'd chosen, and others knew the truth
   had been spoken
and began speaking about their rooms,

their hiding places, but the car kept coming
   up, the car in motion,
music filling it, and sometimes one other person

who understood the bright altar of the dashboard
   and how far away
a car could take him from the need

to speak, or to answer, the key
   in having a key
and putting it in, and going.

Finally, no longer able to abide the sacred
   so defiled,
a young woman said it was God

and only God who filled her with awe,
   and how sad it was
that a dumb car could replace church

in someone's life. The class grew silent again
   as if a hypnotist
had spoken one of those deep, simple words

that jerk people into the past. Maybe a place
   wasn't sacred, one of them said,
if it didn't make you feel uplifted

and small, a little afraid to be in it.
   There were murmurs and nods.
The teacher was pleased that the sacred

seemed disturbingly loose in the room,
   the class divided, alert.
Through the window he could see students

lying on the grass, a Frisbee hovering
   in numinous flight, but in fact
his mind was drifting even farther

to a place he loved where the bartender
   knew his name
and what he liked. The sacred was finished

now, he joked, class was over and everyone
   should think
about what it really meant. The serious student

already knew, and was first out the door.
   Some lingered a bit
to pursue what had been said, though this

was their way of connecting with others
   who might love them
and invite them places they'd never regret.

Oranges

The first time I walked
With a girl, I was twelve,
Cold, and weighted down
With two oranges in my jacket.
December. Frost cracking
Beneath my steps, my breath
Before me, then gone,
As I walked toward
Her house, the one whose
Porch light burned yellow
Night and day, in any weather.
A dog barked at me, until
She came out pulling
At her gloves, face bright
With rouge. I smiled,
Touched her shoulder, and led
Her down the street, across
A used car lot and a line
Of newly planted trees,
Until we were breathing
Before a drugstore. We
Entered, the tiny bell
Bringing a saleslady
Down a narrow aisle of goods
I turned to the candies
Tiered like bleachers,
And asked what she wanted—
Light in her eyes, a smile
Starting at the corners
Of her mouth. I fingered
A nickel in my pocket,
And when she lifted a chocolate
That cost a dime,
I didn't say anything.

I took the nickel from
My pocket, then an orange,
And set them quietly on
The counter. When I looked up,
The lady's eyes met mine,
And held them, knowing
Very well what it was all
About.

   Outside,
A few cars hissing past,
Fog hanging like old
Coats between the trees.
I took my girl's hand
In mine for two blocks,
Then released it to let
Her unwrap the chocolate.
I peeled my orange
That was so bright against
The gray of December
That, from some distance,
Someone might have thought
I was making a fire in my hands.

Early Love

For Emma

Your skin was blue-
puddled snow, I mean
so fine I could trace
your flow from every
tributary. Your breasts,
yes, they were truthful,
freckled and new
beneath your shirt
that summer afternoon
we climbed the ladder
to the barn's dark loft.
We lay down
in the sweet straw
your body
granting the darkness
such mercy
until your brother,
shouting,
brought us down
to fish for crawdads
below the garden.
Your brother,
and your dead sister,
forever between us.
To be with you
I had to pretend
your brother
was my close friend.
On summer nights
we three slept on the lawn
beneath the open sky,
your brother

the dark body
in the center,
we, like wings,
never touching,
unless
I would fling
one arm
in a long arc
across the sky,
perhaps I saw a meteor,
my descending hand
brushing your shoulder,
and you would laugh
and touch my hair
in tender retaliation.
I suppose
you were lonely,
put up with us,
with me
who tugged at you,
innocent and severe,
wanting your skin
to grow around me.
Then your older sister
married and died
within the year.
After the funeral
her husband came for you,
claimed you
from your father
as if you were payment
for that death.
You were sixteen
the day you were taken
by a man in a straw hat
straight-backed
your arms full
of folded clothes
on the front seat
of his car.

I could see everything
from the south pasture
where I lay
tear-shaken, spying
on your leaving,
your solemn descent
from view. I never again
slept with your brother.

Summer Killer

All August we thrilled to rumors.
Near the brook Alex Hunt glimpsed a figure,
ragged and stooping to drink,
and left his flyrod to run two miles
and report. Rewards were waiting,
enough to buy twenty rods.
Lovers on East Hill saw a shadow
flit through headlit brush. She barely
had time to pull up her pants before
they spun into Carl's Garage with the news.
The next day she said she wasn't sure,
"Might've been a bear or a deer,"
and whenever they stopped at the bar
someone was bound to say, "Seen
anything bare-like?" until it ended
in a fight. The State Police parked all day
and night by the entrance to trails
or old wood roads, smoking, eating the snacks
we brought. Four of them got lost on Hedgehog
chasing a barefoot hiker (no shoes sounded suspicious),
but we found them scattered like lost calves, bellowing.

After the first two weeks we thought
we didn't care; but he raised the ante
on every gesture we made, filled the casual
afternoons or evenings with bright contrasts.
You couldn't ignore what passed in the corners of your eyes,
might pause lifting a stick of wood
to listen to crickets, the downward swirl
of a hermit thrush as if someone else
were listening beside you, listening harder
than you ever could. Because he'd killed—
tearing the fabric of every day to stand on the other side,
making it hard to know if he was the substance

casting a shadow that was you, or vice versa.
"Two more loads at least before you go,"
my dad said, and wheeling the barrow back, I shivered,
unwilling to admit how even the drabbest chores
took on gravity, how even nagging
couldn't root out the beauty of danger.

What innocence, I can't help thinking now.
He'd only performed the simplest mayhem,
our killer trapped in a summer home.
Drunk on the liquor of absent owners,
he didn't think before he fired
and blew off the side of one cop's head,
left the other to bleed to death with wounded belly.
Because they were cops and both had families
the Governor called it *A Heinous Crime*
and expanded our vocabulary.
We lowered the town hall flag to halfmast,
bought out all the shells at the hardware
left from last hunting season.
"He's in those woods for sure,"
our senator told us, "we'll have him,"
forgetting those woods spread from Champlain to Erie
if you crossed the fields at night.
Who could believe me now if I said
each one of us dreamed of crouching behind a boulder
in wet moss, stumbling across bogs at dawn, dogs
on the neighboring ridge yapping from footstep
to footstep as we looked for the hidden exit?

But I had my own furtive plans
that nothing could change, so after the firewood
was loosely stacked in its box,
after the keys were handed over,
I picked up the bottle I'd stashed
in the hole of the gatepost and drove
to the house where her parents
had left her in glorious isolation
for the whole night while they journeyed
to Boston. What more could you ask for?

A house made for summer only, as rustic
as any movie set, a fireplace where two hogs
could have twirled on spits,
and a bear rug as soft as a feathery bed.

Of course we'd pretended we weren't going here,
bare in the firelight, the owls outside
hooting us on, our young bodies knowing more
than their owners could ever have guessed.
If it hurt for a moment, she didn't complain,
and after the silence, after we heard the house
settle down to the cooler night air
she brought in a blanket so we could lie naked
breathing and whispering and drinking the whiskey
that turned our dizzy words liquid
before we went back to our learning.

What instinct made me leave the car
down the road? I came like a thief
to my lover's house, and praised myself
for that salvation. "Wasn't that Willy's car
in the field?" I heard her old man ask
as I crouched naked on the screened-in porch.
"I doubt it," she murmured, trying so hard
to keep those syllables firm. "What
in the world are you bundled like that for?"
her mother asked shrilly. She must have been lumped
like a squaw in that blanket, my clothes
and hers clutched to her body. "I'm naked,"
she snapped, and after her angry heels pummeled
the floor, those small feet flapping
up the stairs, her father, his own tongue slurring,
muttered, "Clara, I'll never understand my daughter."

That wasn't my problem. I dreaded
the sudden flick of a light, his need
to come out and look at the stars. He poked
at the fire, she asked for a drink,
and slowly I pushed out the screen, blessing

its rot and the way it tore easily
out of the frame. "Honey," she was calling,
"did you hear something out there?"
but I wasn't waiting, hung by my fingers
and prayed as I tried to remember
how close to the cliff their house was perched,
and dropped. Not far, but my knees
buckled me flat on my ass, enough to imbed
pebbles there. I was moving into the trees
away from cliffs when the light went on
and she began screaming, "He's here,
he's here, he tried to break in."

I won't tell you what my feet looked like
after five miles of hiking away from the roads,
scratches all over my body from alders
and spruce boughs. I circled our house
for hours with my clouds of mosquitoes
waiting for parents to fall asleep,
cursing my father's insomnia.
The phone should have rung or police have arrived
in search of the ripper of screens, despoiler
of daughters. I hunched by the woodshed,
my knees to my chest, my back surrendered to bloodsuckers.
Stars were blinking in layers, I shivered
in rhythm to the quivering sheets of aurora.
I had to wonder if all this was worth it,
but no matter how numb the punished body,
I answered I'd do it again and again
even if she weren't the one,
and couldn't help praising beginnings.

The last night went out and I stood
and someone stood with me. Or at least
that's what my eyes were telling,
but wherever I looked directly
nothing was there, only tree trunks
and shadows. I moved, and he moved
with me, I stopped and he waited.

The dark house was mine for the taking,
but the whole world spread out and held up the sky.
We could have kept walking together,
not seeing each other. We chose
to part at the door to the cottage
and I'm sure he nodded, I waved,
and I would have spoken except I knew
we would follow each other forever
through woods and fields and streets of strange cities.

I answered all riddles. The car had run out of gas,
that bundle of clothes had been left at her house after tennis.
"We've had such a scare," her mother told mine.
"That killer, we're sure he was trying
to break in and rob us and think
what might have happened if we hadn't come home,
but stayed in Boston." She and I
never had chances like that again.
The summer ended, as usual, in tears,
a season's passing mourned for that moment,
but how could I grieve for long?
I'd gotten away with all I had wanted.

They found him that winter in Arizona.
He'd taken to bragging in barrooms.
They put him away, didn't kill him.
I kept my mouth shut so they never found me,
and still I'm taking whatever I can,
hoping I won't have to shoot my way out,
and trying before I leave each house
to give everything back.

White

1964 and I'm parked
in my father's sports car
with Kathy Quigley,
it's late August
in Santa Barbara and
the moonsoaked foothills
simmer from the day's heat.
The top's down and finally,
without a word,
my hands sail
past the petticoat
and three clasps of the bra . . .
perspiration beads
on my clean-shaven lip,
the lemon blossoms
anoint the air;
we swear this is love
and burn beneath our stars.

13 years and despite the loss
of orchards, the advance of homes,
kids still park out here
and throw their car doors open
to the high bleached grass of summer.
In an old Rambler
I light a cigarette
and wait for the moonrise
over La Cumbre Peak
like a host elevated by the priest
during Mass—I'd look for you then
amid a landscape of Catholic blouses . . .

And because my hands are blank
as this foothill shale,
because there is a moon,
I remember you
girl-like and eager as light.

Yet I'm content
without the life of averages
our parting spared me,
with whatever song
for my pockets month to month.
Tonight, under the stars
and all their thorns,
I no longer swear love
or know the misery—
I am blessed, purely
by the first memory
of your breasts,
by the simple grace
of what was here—
the lemon blossoms,
the white heart
of what we were.

Almost Dancing

In this kind of wind
blowing hard from the west—
sloughed off the Pacific
to dust the desert floor,
collecting all that chaff and grit
and whatever else a wind needs
to huff headlong into these mountains—
even the half-dead, loblolly pines
bow a bit from their stiff waists,
begin to dip and sway;
their boughs nodding together
like the heads of drunks
who have nowhere to go
between last call and their dark, bolted homes—
the last bars of a two-bit song
blowing from the jukebox—
almost touching because of the beat,
almost dancing . . .

I was the kid with two left feet
in a school where most of my classmates
majored in meanness
and the stupefying logarithms of sex.
I held up the wall at the senior prom
while the other kids grooved
and ground their groins
like interchangeable parts
in some competent, well-lubed machine.
Even the chaperones shuffled their feet.
Even the sober, undrinkable punch
shimmered like a little sea.
The band played poorly on secondhand instruments
they'd eventually trade

for bus tickets out of town.
I would have left
if I had known where to go.
I would have danced if anyone had asked me.

How simple it looks out there
from in here: back and forth, to and fro.
Not the old-fashioned boxstep exactly,
but some facile choreography
starting low in the roots
and welling up through the trunk,
branches and twigs of every green
and once-green thing.
Likewise the beer cans dumped by the road
and the stop sign on its one metal leg
stir to the vagrant music of March—
the whole world a dancehall
for whatever moves with ease.
How simple it looks out there,
and yet—
what's here to move me to unlock the door,
unlock my bones some
and take the first step?

What's here to move me back
to the N.C.O. Club in Selma, Alabama—
nineteen-seventy-whatever-it-was—
where I sat with my parents
listening to the Ink Spots,
a band fallen to low-rent gigs
for homesick GI's
and blowzy town-girls no one would marry?
It was the first time we got family drunk
and when the game-legged guitarist
kicked the group into "Maybe,"
that graying, corpulent couple
who'd brought me up
breezed to the center of the empty floor
and fell into each other

like falling in love—
dancing so lightly I held my breath,
afraid they'd blow away.

I'd never seen them move like that—
so many moves I've missed.
So many steps I might have learned
by stepping with my wooden feet
into the fanfare of the world,
to let its music play me green.
Maybe the wind that whips these walls,
drums the glass
and whistles down the chimney pipe
could find me with its restless riffs—
take my breath away I mean—
and lead me from myself;
a lithe wind,
a measureless wind
alive with its grace notes of seed and decay,
leading nowhere
I could follow for long,
leading away . . .

Ghost Story

I've found three people now who claim they've seen
the girl's ghost underneath the apple tree
where she last met her lover on the night
he strangled her. Sue is upset with me:
she says things need repair around the house;
a grown man shouldn't waste his time asking
about ghosts. You know, Mom, that I don't believe
in ghosts, but she's become a legend here;
her murder gave the farmers something besides
planting to talk about. As you'd expect,
the girl was beautiful—with straight, black hair
that caught the moonlight like a summer lake;
astonished, dark-brown eyes; and skin so pale
some people wondered if she might be ill.
But no one could describe the boy, except
he lisped. The girl was pregnant when she died,
and everyone is sure he murdered her,
although he disappeared from town without
a fingerprint to make it certain he
was *there* that night. Her being pregnant doesn't
seem to me sufficient proof, and yet
it's also said the boy refused to help
his father with the milking chores. Three nights
I hid behind the old, stone orchard wall
to watch the apple tree, not expecting
truly to see her ghost, yet trying to
imagine her actually as she stood
there waiting for her lover to appear.
The third night someone came—a man, I'd say
about my height and build, and carrying
a stick or rifle, maybe hunting for
raccoons; or else her sleepless father might
have wandered through the orchard wishing to

out-walk his grief. I called to him. At first,
as if expecting me, he looked around,
then ran across the orchard to the woods.
Sue says I'm lucky that he didn't shoot.

   Sue doesn't know I've come to talk to you.
The difference between Dad's books and what
the farmers saw is only that Dad knows
his characters exist as words. Explain
to Sue all *his* inventions are just ghosts!
And yet I wanted Sue to understand
the real fear that girl felt. Picture her face!—
that's what I should have said—surely someone
might have perceived the danger she was in,
and tried to rescue her. That's what her father
should have done—or else some neighbor's boy
who loved her, though she had rejected him.
And if I write her history, at least
her memory will live—if not her child.

   I'll get the details right—the scudding clouds,
the apple trees in rows, a piled stone wall,
the lacy, sleeveless dress that showed her arms.
But whom should I include—her father, Sue,
both you and Dad, a neighbor's boy, myself?
Sue's almost got to see her underneath
the apple tree in August moonlight, fear
on her hushed face, the shaded flowing
of her silver arms, a cameo around
her thin, tense throat, maybe just like the one
you always wear, engraved with circling whales,
that has my tinted portrait tucked inside.

Still Life

Jogging out of a stand of pin oak and
juniper in the morning fog, I came upon
a six-point buck beside a wire fence,
still wet with yesterday's rain,
a poacher's dropping protruding
from a black plastic bag, forelegs
running, like a perverse sculpture
or a Neanderthal cave drawing
or one I had seen earlier poised
and ready to slip away at my next
step. Except the dead one, as
still as the other, head cocked
against a limestone rock, was looking
curiously at me, in wonderment
still, at point blank range.
But it was me this time who twitched
and quickly moved on down the path
without looking back, thinking how life
reduces, after all.

Unlike the time when I was eleven and
found the old ragman Morelli lying across
a railroad track: body on one side,
head on the other, as though he had just
waited, knowing what he was doing,
not moving, even as the train
ran him over, as though he were posing,
thinking ahead to those who might
find him there, or to newsphotos.
But it was only me to register
the first human response to his gesture,
only me, who never spoke a real word to
him, who hung on the back of his wagon,
grinning while he yelled in broken

English and threatened with his whip,
too old to frighten, too old to hurt.
And here I was again, looking at him
unafraid, strangely clinical, as though
he were a lab specimen in formaldehyde,
fascinated with the cauterized cut, with
his stillness, with death, with the first
death of one I had actually known living,
and the stillness of the scene, perfectly
lighted in the early morning sun,
a professional photograph
of a small boy and his shadow
astride a quiet railroad track,
aware of the summer warmth
and the smells of slick metal and sumac
and the unexpected greenness on the rail
between head and body.
But that didn't finish it that summer,
because later on, on a terribly hot day
when the smell of tar and creosote hung
heavy, I saw another body under
a stack of railroad ties and stuck it
hard in the side with a stick, kicking
the bottoms of its feet to be sure.
When it didn't move, I ran down the track
to tell a New York Central crew
and brought them running. They had barely
pushed the ties aside, when a big black
wino raised up from his sweating sleep,
like a hippopotamus exploding
from a river bottom, cursing the sun
and the heat and the railroad crew,
shaking hell out of me and running me
back to the neighborhood without much
to talk about that time. I guess Death
had his little joke.

Then, when I was forty, you died.
The same year we talked. I mean
the time outside by the old Plymouth

when you were in your sixty-seventh
summer and I asked you how you felt
inside and you said the same as when
you were twenty-seven. You said
that was the whole thing about getting
old. The mismatch between inside and out.
You watch yourself dying with young eyes.
We were looking right at each other,
right into each other, not at our shoes
or down the street, and we were talking
about ourselves, not sports, not gardens.
And I was ashamed to discover how long
it had taken to recognize my father
as a whole person apart from my father.
Right after that I got the job out west
and you were gone.

When I first saw you, we alone,
me before the others,
in the stillness of the scene,
perfectly lighted, suspended in scents
of gardenia and formaldehyde, I thought
that I was in the wrong room viewing
a waxen figure made to resemble you,
that wasn't you, that was Morelli
beside the railroad track, that became
a dead deer in a bag, that was a man
under railroad ties who would not rise.
Our eyes could not touch. My insides
were waxen, my brain the photograph
of a small boy and his shadow
frozen forever in the summer sun.
Still life. Still life. Still life.

Autumnal Equinox

When summer starts to fall,
when the hay sits in the
field like loaves of bread
left by some giant to cool,

we start to gather the shocks.
Mornings begin with biscuits and flour gravy.
The paper is sliced with ritual—
News, market, Abby, patterns, and funnies.
I get the ads, studying them with
the same intensity as my father
studies the hog futures.

In between the help wanted
and motorcycle ads,
I always take the extra biscuits
and sausage patties.
After each Honda ad I slice a biscuit.
After each Yamaha ad I insert a patty.
A sandwich game—sometimes equaling
more patties than biscuits
or empty halves.

By the time I finish my game, I wrap up
the leftovers in a square of waxed paper
left under my plate by Mom every morning,
and then read the leftover news.

I catch another hot day,
a story about the Packers,
the report of a convict, escaped
from Swisher County Jail,
shot in his flight.

I hear the horn honk
on the '56 pickup truck.
Race to read Dick Tracy.
Horn honks twice, I grab my
waxed paper makeshift bag,
handkerchief, an old straw hat.
As the screen slams twice
I yell, "Bye—I'm coming,"
in the same breath.

Older brothers and Dad sit in the
cab—half angry, half joking,
"Damn boy readin' those funny papers."

They talk about this year's crop,
imagine the hot work ahead. I talk
on my make-believe wrist radio. Tell
Sam, "Keep 'em covered, we're on our
way." And imagine the crimes in the field.

Arriving, we find our individual tasks
as naturally as the bees find theirs in
Mom's garden. Dad drives the tractor,
Brother, the oldest, stands on the trailer
ready to catch the shock Junior throws him.
Junior and I walk tight-rope style down
the furrows carved last spring.

I get to run ahead of Dad and tractor.
Kicking over the bundles so Junior
can pick up and toss.

I fight each Halloween symbol,
winning freedom or capturing some
hardened criminal for Dick Tracy.
Sometimes I play Dick too. Some
get a simple shove, others get a
farm boy's judo kick—each tumble
in the line according to my duties
and the crime.

Near the end of the row—
not far from the Farm-to-Market road,
I spy the escaped convict.

He is at least 3 or 4 bundles
ahead and has a bazooka.
I hide behind the shocks and
he keeps shooting them down.
Making me run to the next one.
Closer.
Desperate moves in a hot field.

I see my chance when he is distracted
by a patrol car passing down the other side.
I spring.
I tackle.

My make-believe capture halts.
A smell—one I know—a dead animal.
I roll over,
clear the hay from my face and see
two eyes resting evenly across from mine.

Blood stains the hay near my hand;
I scream.
Dad, Brother, and Junior come running.
Dad yells, "I thought I told you to
stop playing around and be careful."
When they reach me, the dead man, and
the shock—three parallel lines,
a policeman's lineup,
they just stand there.

Junior throws up,
Brother curses,
Dad reaches down, pulls me
by my ankles.

As I slide away
I see where the skin mixes with blood,

sticks to the ground and insects play
"Cops and Robbers" in and out of the
decaying spaces. The skin pulls away
from the face and I remember the plastic
wrappers and how they melt when I burn
the garbage. Another game I play while
grownups watch the nightly news.

He is a dead man
in my field of villains and heroes.
A convict who sandwiched himself
in—between the hay—a shock.
I remember thinking, "Like my sausage patty.
Back in the truck, all wrapped up."
He hadn't meant to die here on my turf.
I hadn't meant to find him.
I knew there was a convict there,
but not a real one, not a dead one.

The next morning, I leave the waxed paper
under my plate, tell Mom, "I'll eat for lunch
what you fix for Dad, Brother, and Junior."
Read the story about the boy who found
the convict.
Untouched, the funnies stay wedged somewhere
between the plate of biscuits and the
platter of sausage patties.

Pushing my chair back, I stride to the
door, say "bye" on the first slam.

At the pickup, I turn over a pail and
straddle. Wait. Imagine the work ahead.
Shifting, I pull my collar up
against the chill.

The Shriving

And the seventh angel poured
out his vial into the air.

Revelation 16:17

He was a druggist. The storefront building
had one long room with a pressed-tin ceiling,
a line of revolving fans down the middle,
and random-oak floors darkened with polishing.
The soda-fountain counter was a slab
of black glass chipped with tiny moons.
There were tables and chairs made of wire
where you brought your date after a game:
you could look up and see yourself in the mirror.
The boys who worked there had imported brooms
with handles maybe ten feet long or more;
once each week they had to sweep the ceiling.
When the brooms wore out, the druggist took them,
saved them for a time when he burnt the worms.

Save for the times when he burnt the worms,
I never saw him smile. If those who lived there
had a name for sacred, they never said it aloud.
Once when I was small the aunties took me out
to a grove of walnut trees with nothing else
around them, no green thing strong enough
to rise up from that ground. Some called it
poison, others spoke of a strange power
in the earth itself, which the tree could summon.
My morning there, gathering nuts—black
clinkers—stained my fingers for weeks after.
And from my first glimpse of that place I knew
there are some things not written in books,
there are some trees whose names you know on sight.

These are the names of the trees I came to know:
willow, which is first to turn green in springtime,
poplar, which looks silver when the wind blows,
oak, which is always last to let go of its leaves.
Each time he turned the car into the lane
he praised the walnut trees that stood there:
how they would bring a fortune at the mill,
how their heartwood, sliced thin as paper,
would unfold like ripples in a stream.
But they were his possessions now, they came
with the house; he aimed to see they lived out
their span. When the first moths arrived
and spread their stickiness through the trees,
he began to sweat, to cry out in his sleep.

Those who talked in their sleep, who could not rest,
came to the store each day to visit the druggist,
waited in line for a chance to say what was wrong.
Wednesday afternoons he closed, like the bank,
and stayed in the back room, counting the stock.
He knew she would be lounging on the bedclothes,
talking to some drummer who stands by the door,
who wants a cigarette now but lacks the nerve
to light one up. She would tell about her husband,
how he killed moths and butterflies in a jar.
The man would begin pulling on his pants.
The druggist tilts a line of pills into a box,
tells the boys to be sure and sweep the ceiling,
he is going home, there are chores to do.

Going home after practice, doing the chores—
those things kept me busy. When the war started
the state widened the road to four lanes,
chopped down the trees in front of his house.
But even before that, when he first retired,
and she was long dead, of some illness,
and I, his grand-nephew, was left there
on summer mornings, for him to look after—
even then I guessed at what had happened:

when he would gather up the old tools
and get a worn-out broom down from the loft
and go out to burn the caterpillar nests
where they clotted the trees. When I watched him
make harsh changes in the way things were.

Change made him harsh. Things got in the way
of what he saw and heard. It took a long time
for him to tie the rags about the broom,
soak them in oil, then strike a match
and hoist the fuming torch into the air,
touching it here and there among the leaves
where moths were dreaming. I saw them burst
and fall in a bright rain against the grass.
And when the trees were purged, and he stood
with hair and eyebrows full of soot, calling,
pointing toward the branches, saying how
they were safe now, the fire had healed them,
and when I grew up, I could do it too—
I knew she was not dead, she had run away.

I learned one does not run away from death:
it comes like a harsh glare billowing darkness.
When I went back, after the war, and stopped
at the café next to the bank, no one there
remembered me, though they recalled his name.
"He drove his car onto the tracks one night,"
a farmer said. "Those Nickel Plate tracks
are gone now, all the way to Windfall.
You can hunt rabbit on the old right-of-way
and not worry about some train hitting you.
That whole stretch has come up in wild cherry;
last year the trees were thick with moths."
"I remember him now," the feedstore man said.
"He was a druggist. Had a storefront building."

51

Maud

You and Nell found Aunt Maud
stretched on a cot
in her farmhouse,
five or six dogs piled on top,
and to carry the body out
you plunked down boards
so your feet wouldn't sink
through the ankle-deep poop.
I remember Maud's place—
the narrow path that led
through the three-room shack,
the piles of books and Des Moines *Registers*,
the Wonder Bread wrappers
folded and stacked to the ceiling,
braided into rugs on the floor.
Slices were toasted on top
the cookstove, then spread
with peanut butter.
Slices were dipped in milk and egg,
fried, and drowned in maple syrup.
Slices were crumbled and scattered
in the snow for the juncos,
were broken into a bowl
for the dogs, tossed whole
to the hogs in the barn.
When Nell and I visited,
we bounced down the lane, rolling
up the windows, the dogs
charging the car, tails down,
teeth set in a sneer.
Nell honked and Maud shuffled
out on the porch, shouting,
"Here, Prince."

(Maud had a string of seven
different dogs named Prince.)
"Don't know what's gotten
into that dog."
I swung open the car door
and the pack sniffed and licked
my pant leg until I scurried into
the house, where Nell and I
teetered from one leg to the other
in the tiny kitchen—
there wasn't a chair to sit—
and Maud pulled out a piece
of her moldy bread and
offered us grilled cheese.
"Believe I'll pass," Nell said.

I remember Maud's place
but you say that was only the last.
As she grew older and richer,
flesh puffing from frame,
she moved again and again,
each house smaller and shabbier,
further from town,
each house taking in one more dog.
"Here, Prince," she called,
hoisting herself into her jeep,
the pack squeezed in around her,
drooling on the seats,
the dash, her canvas cape
that flapped in the wind
as she raced down the gravel road
and roared into your drive
to collect the rent.
(Grandpa had left her twenty acres
and soon twenty grew to eighty
to half the county
and she charged you
to live on the home place.)
Prince snapped at your hand

as Maud huffed and groaned
and pried herself out from
behind the wheel, her cape hiking up
just enough for you to see
that underneath she was naked.

Home, she hosed down the cape
and hung it over the porch railing
where every Sunday morning
she picked up her copy of
The New York Times,
and in the afternoon lay
on her cot and sang along
with the radio,
squeaking out the arias
and recitatives
with the singers from the Met.
Once, at nineteen she married
and ran off to Chicago
with a fertilizer salesman,
but came back in six months,
claiming the city unsafe.
(But Grandma said that's where
she picked up all her Eastern airs.)
Once, Prince trembled when Maud
whistled him into her jeep
for their daily trip to town.
He hid under the porch steps
and the rest of the pack
closed round, so Maud choked
the engine and left them behind,
zooming toward town, running
her usual stop sign,
rounding Kussell's corner,
never looking left nor right at the tracks.
Suddenly, she was in the air,
rising, floating,
her body light as if full of holes.
Then she was punched down

again into her jeep,
the train still blasting its horn,
and she felt her wind rush out,
lungs fold in, her leg snap.
After that, she dragged one foot
as she hobbled around the shack,
and what was left of the jeep
sank into the mud down by the creek.
She quit going
to church but made the priest
ride out every First Friday
with the sacrament. Things were
in English by then,
and when Father Maloy held
the host in front of her face—
"This is my Body"—
she refused to say, "Amen."
You drove there
with the rent check and sometimes
found the two dark eyes
of a shotgun aimed out the window,
or sometimes you found Maud
on the tractor in the field,
circling round and round,
neither plowing nor planting,
the sun beating down on her naked back.
Once, you found her sitting
cross-legged on the cot, eyes fixed.
She didn't hear you come in.
She didn't even blink
when you put your hand on her arm.
She just began to talk.

MAUD:
There was a ewe killed down at old man
Sullivan's place. He came knocking saying
a pack of neighbor dogs done it and
would I help him round them up.
I fetched my gun then we headed off

to Burke's and took care of Old Shep.
Then to Kunkle's and Kussell's and Fink's,
but when we got to Mammy Flannery's,
she swore up and down that her little
rat terrier ain't done nothing.
"Oh," she wailed, "not him, not him."
She begged and begged me but Sullivan
already had him cornered in the barn
and Mammy fell to a pool at my feet
when she heard the shot. Then I headed home.
And found Prince.
Oh, he done it all right. Still had
the blood dribbling down his chin.
But up until then he was the best I'd ever had.
I trained that Prince.
I taught him to come and sit and heel,
and then he used to be my dishwasher.
I'd put my plate down on the floor and
lickety-split, it'd be clean.
In the morning I'd poke my head out
the window and holler, "Prince,"
and he'd come wagging and I'd want
a certain sow and all I had to do was point
and Prince'd nose her out. But I took him
down by the creek and set him up on the bank.
Jesus. He perched up there just-a-grinning,
his ears pointing as I raised my gun.
Well, there's one thing.
I should've dug the hole first.
I should've dug the hole first.

When they dug Maud's hole,
they went way down toward the end,
clear of everyone, and the priest
said that's where she belonged,
willing all her money to her dogs.
And when they lowered her in,
no one knew how long she'd been gone.
She didn't believe in a phone

and would go for weeks without
seeing a person.
At the wake they kept
the coffin lid shut and
you never told anyone what you
found that day you stepped
on the porch, the dogs whining,
bowls empty, ribs sticking out.
You knew by the stench,
but never told how you covered
your face with a handkerchief
when you and Nell bent over the body,
and how the body had turned black,
as if a stain had spread over the skin,
and how the hands were folded across
the chest and little bits of flesh
on the fingertips were nibbled away
like crumbs of bread.

Something Left to Say

For my Mother (1918–1972)

That night I was not there,
and for a moment somehow you returned
from weeks of nothing
but wanderings in your head.
You came clearly with something left to say.
They said you opened your eyes,
knew the room well.
I knew my absence well;
how I could not stand by only breathing
in that sick-dark room,
you settling
deeper in the four-poster
under its canopy of roses.

Now at every window, through
white summer hats,
through candlelight shining in my hair,
voices whisper: *stay.*
Outside the mockingbird goes on
with his frail-throated song.
Your final words are repeated
like a sharp wind that's never left
my back. They told me how you called
my name, looked around. And looked.

Celestial

To end this day
I shoot the black calf,
down so long
she would never rise,
so weak there is no
last shiver but mine.

In the ring of pines
off the highway I leave her,
poor hide and bones,
almost breathing.
Rank sacks of garbage
and yellow smoke roll
before a wind too sharp
for the flawless sky.

To end this day I wait
for a sign to release me.
In the waste I stand watch
with the spectacular sun,
the small, bone-white moon.
As if expecting words
I do not have, they lie
low on either horizon, each
round as the calf's round eye.

The Dog Poisoner

To this day, no one knows who he was or she was.
All we kids knew was that it came in the night,
little balls of hamburger (Then you could buy it,
three pounds for a quarter. My mother made me tell
the butcher it was for my dog, but we ate it.)
came over the fence, lay there and real soon
a dog lay there, writhing in pain. Ground glass

was all it ever used and we hated it, would I'm sure
have killed it if we could ever have caught it.
Forgive me for saying "it," but who could think
of such a creature as an animal or even a human?
My mother said once what it really wanted was to kill
a human, a boy or a girl, but hadn't enough courage.

We boys finally banded together and patrolled the huge
vacant lots that separated our homes but all we ever
got was tired and our parents made us stop, even though
the killings went on.
                      One day they just quit. It happened
that the day before an old man who lived down towards
the Valley got sick and died, vomiting blood.
The doc said he didn't know what killed him
but we did. He got his hamburger mixed up and
God forgive me, we were so glad we got out
and danced in a circle, shouting as if it were
raining or some other miracle had happened.

Cottontail

A couple of kids,
we went hunting for woodchucks
fifty years ago
in a farmer's field.
No woodchucks
but we cornered
a terrified
little cottontail rabbit
in the angle
of two stone fences.
He was sitting up,
front paws together,
supplicating,
trembling,
while we were deciding
whether to shoot him
or spare him.
I shot first
but missed,
thank God.
Then my friend fired
and killed him
and burst into tears.
I did too.
A little cottontail.
A haunter.

The Chicken Poem

Every farmyard in Nebraska
is haunted by the presence
of a barred rock rooster.
He's a ghost, of course,
because his species is extinct,
but this doesn't prevent him
from standing down there
by the stock tank, weighing
ten pounds, black and white,
in the garb of a convict.
And he's tough. I mean
he's meaner than skunk meat.
His comb is ripped up from
attacking his galvanized reflection
in the hog pans; he's so choleric
he won't drop either wing
to a hen; and he's been that way
for life. When just a few
hours old, he chewed the fuzz
from the leghorn chicks,
turning them pitiably
into featherless bipeds.
And three or four days later,
attacking again, he deflowered
every pullet in the barn.
Then he graduated,
lying in wait for men.
People like the Necchi-Elna
salesman, or the woman
who sold Watkins Products.
Attacking their shins,
or just running at them,
low over the lawn, his anus
on fire like a V-2 bomb.

This is why out here
we have our own terror.
Because no barred rock rooster,
dying, ever went to heaven.
Once dead, he simply came
back down, taking evil as his good.
Ask hired men who know
what it is to watch ghosts
rising from their dusting places
among the lilacs. Ask
salesmen who keep their cars
running in the yard. Or watch
the pathetic nervousness
of grown dogs. And pity,
above all, those poor Avon women—
delicate souls who approach
the house knowing a chicken
is about to flog a runner
in their hose. But watch
these dear little ladies arm
themselves with whatever they can:
aftershaves, wet lipsticks,
or more appropriate yet,
those little white jars
of vanishing cream.

The Bat in the Bedroom

Was it there at all,
the bat whose leathery,
extended wing
we thought we saw hanging
from the cat's mouth?
And when one of us yelled,
didn't the cat run off,
leaving hell's image
to flap around the room
and bounce against the mirror?
But under the blanket
we trapped it with,
no impression, no movement.
Only our lightest
prodding with a broom
discovered a squeaking
like a broken appliance.
We called the police.
"Take a broom," they said,
"and smash it." But we
had no heart for the obvious.
We put on our garden gloves,
and using a dust pan and notebook
we enfolded it in still
more blankets and sheets.
We threw the bundle into the air
outside the house, but
from its unravelling
saw nothing, nothing at all,
escape. What
must the neighbors think
to see us on the porch
with our arms raised toward heaven

while all around us
the life of our bed
floats down like parachutes
people have fallen from.

Close to Home

I saw the snake again at dusk
lying on the road. I had not known
I was walking up to him. I figured
I was just walking along. But he lay there
like an unfinished thought,
not coiled, but with the randomness
of something dropped from a height,
a big snake. The ground was deciding him
where he lay, snake-limp, yet snake-alert,
in the calm with which things from below
are always alive to light,
even at dusk. As I came close
to see his black and yellow markings,
he took on that swirl behind his head
(this is how snakes frown), his body
flinching into the waviness
that, reacting to threat,
looks like a threat. I felt my own neck bristle,
the dog part of me. He flickered his black tongue
as if jotting a note in the air
and I saw that his slick head
was oval, probably not poisonous.
I remembered the man who said,
"I never ask 'em their pedigree. If it's
a snake, I just kill 'em." I thought
of my father, who had to stop the car
on any country road and take out
across the field with a stick.
At this moment the snake began to unshrug
the wad of himself, crossing
the road like a spill. My dog neck went down.
It's not true that snakes crawling
make no sound, but they don't make much.

When he had disappeared, the road came back,
though it was not quite the same road.
At nine o'clock I don't feel virtuous
when I think of him a quarter-mile away,
but the woods seem richer with a snake in them
yellow and black, a sliding night
that carries the day on its back,
lighting up some of the dark places.

A Victory

Certain acts survive. I recall
one rural Georgia scene:
the cottonmouth that abandoned
the Flint River bottom
to inhabit the cotton field
and sleep among dry weevils
inherited the hoe's steel
blade arcing across the sun.
Grandma clove the moccasin,
declaring under her homespun bonnet,
"There, sir. Serves you right."
The black spade head
yawned a coffin's satin,
thrust fangs in dirt,
shot the tongue's
impotent lightning.
The dusty muscle whipped
as she bent, then rose.
Amid arid furrows and snowball
cotton, she brandished
weapon and victim in her bare
harvest hands, straddled the row
and shouted with ardor,
"Got one!" Shouted, "Mine!"
Wasp-waisted cousins,
red-fleshed with June and joyous,
danced in the field.
One bull groaned at the fence.
Did the irises burst into bloom?

Around the Campfire

Around the campfire we sang hymns.
When asked I'd play my flute, and lay
a melody between night's
incessant cannonfire that boomed
irregularly, but with the depth
of kettle drums. Occasionally,
in lulls, we'd hear a fading snatch
of Yankee song sucked to us in
the backwash of their cannonballs.
These are, oddly enough, fond memories.

One night, a Texas boy sat down
and strummed a homemade banjo.
He'd bought it for a canteen full
of corn. He followed me around
and pestered me to teach him notes.
He loved that ragged box but, Lord,
he couldn't play it worth a damn.
Nobody could. I tried to tell him so.
"Hell, I know, Sid," he said. "If I
were any good, I would worry me
too much. This way I can just blame
the instrument."
                    And this, too, is
a fond instructive memory.

Boom BOOM. "Listen to *that*," he said.
Then silence once again as Yanks
swabbed out the cannonbarrel and rammed
another charge into the gun. They paused
a minute in their work. *Boom BOOM.*
Our cannon fired in answer to
in-coming shells. "Don't they," he asked

"sound like a giant limping through
the woods in search of us?" I laughed.
It was a peaceful night and we
were working on some liquid corn.
Boom BOOM. I filled my cup again
and said, "He's after us all right."
He laughed. *Boom BOOM.* I sloshed more in
his cup. A shell exploded to our right.
A piece of shrapnel nicked my ear,
and when the smoke had cleared, I saw
him sitting, looking for his cup
and for the hand he'd held it in.

From this, I didn't learn a thing.

The Huts at Esquimaux

For Dave Smith

Our clothes are still wet from wading
The Chickamauga last evening.
There is heavy frost. We have
Walked on the dead all night.
Now in the firelight
We are exchanging shells and grape shot.

I can still hear our loud huzza
When late in the day
The enemy fell into full retreat
Along the pine ridge to the East . . .

We chased them until we were weary.
Each night this week
There's been something
To keep me from sleep. Just an hour ago
I saw

A dead sharp-shooter sitting
Against a rock with a scallop
Of biscuit still lodged in his mouth.
He wore one silk sock.

Snediker has returned from Chattanooga
With five thousand convalescents
For the left wing of their musketry.

We have roasted a deer
With a molasses sauce and pepper.
Magrill and Zandt have returned
From horse hunting with a sack of sugar.
By morning we will have buried our dead

And fed the prisoners: Joe Cotton
Will hang all seven of them in one tree
When he sees they're done
Licking their fingers . . .

I shot a Rebel yesterday
In high water just for cursing me.
Just six months ago
For that alone it would have meant
Three days in stockade.

We can see now that cannonading
Has set the hillside on fire.
The wounded Grays
Will be burned
Beyond their Christian names . . .

Joe Cotton says he'd ask God
For rain, but he's got no tent
And river water
Has chilled him straight through

To the very quick of his being.

Postcards of the Hanging: 1869

1.

Clifford, we've grown too far apart.
So yesterday I bought some postal cards
and have resolved to send them all to you.
But what to say? I'm doing well
and Mary says to say she's doing fine.

2.

Remember the large oak beside Hall's barn?
This afternoon I saw a nigger hanged from it
For spitting on a white girl's shoes.
Or so he said. She said he grabbed her breast.
I suspect the truth is somewhere in between.
When he said *shoes*, they went berserk.

3.

Last night, disturbed, I woke at four o'clock.
I'd dreamed but couldn't recollect the dream.
So I got up and studied law
until I smelled the bacon, eggs, and tea,
and ate myself into the solid world.

4.

In church it hit me like a cannonball:
I'd dreamed of feet—such gorgeous feet,
so soft and smooth and dainty pink,
they looked as if they'd never walked on the earth,
as if they were intended just to walk on air.

5.

As far as hangings go, this one was quiet.
By the time they got him to the tree, they'd calmed.
They sat him on a mule and slipped the noose

around his neck. He sang—or started to—
"Swing Low, Sweet Chariot," but lost his place,
and when he paused somebody slapped the mule
across the rump. It wouldn't move,
and finally they had to push the mule
from underneath the colored man.

6.

The bottoms of his boots were not worn through.
Those boots! They kicked and lashed above the mule
and tried to get a purchase on the air
before they stilled and seemed to stand on tip-toe
like another acorn hanging from the oak.

7.

A colored peddler who had stopped to watch
asked them if he could have the dead man's boots.
"He can't use dem, gennelmens," he said.
"And dese ol' boots of mine is shot."
"Why sure, old-timer. Take the boots
and anything else you want off this dead fool."
"I thank ya kindly, gennelmens. Jus' the boots."

8.

I blacked my boots after supper tonight—
walking boots, working boots, Sunday shoes,
and even the cavalry boots I wore
when we were living on horseback in the war.
That Raven was a handsome horse!
When I was through, my hands were black
as the dead man's hands. Even my face was smudged.
Now clean, the boots give off an eerie glow
like a family of cats lined up beside the fire.

9.

Does this make sense to you? This afternoon
I walked five miles into the woods,
sat down in a clearing in the pines,
and sobbed and sobbed until my stomach hurt.

When I stopped, I tied the laces together,
slung the freshly dirty boots around my neck,
and walked, barefooted, home. When I got there
my feet were sticking to the ground with blood.
It helped a bit. I'm doing better now
and Mary says to say she's doing fine.

The Last Man Killed
by Indians
in Kimble County, Texas

Sam Speer, watching the black ball
of a rider growing larger against
the soft morning snow, turned away
long enough to fix the positions
of weapons still in the cabin
and move toward the muzzle loader
propped in the far corner
to his right, his mother stopping
the rhythm of the Christmas dough
and looking to him.

He knew that no one
would make a message run
in that kind of weather
on Christmas Eve day
unless there was trouble.
Serious trouble.
Death and destruction trouble.
Fire, outlaw, rustler,
and Indian trouble.
And Indians were too long overdue.
That he knew in the chill
of last night as he followed
the shadows of the hills
in the moonlight, full and bright,
a Comanche moon just right
for a war dance and travel by night,
and the cattle were restless
in their pasture. The rider
sat his horse like Tom Doran,
and it was he who emerged,

shouting from the raging snow,
crusted in white,
letting his words go
even before
he had pulled the big bay up.

"Isaac Kountz's been murdered
by Indians. Shot dead
from ear to ear through the head.
Nine bucks, renegades,
Comanche maybe,
in white man's clothes,
Sebastian said.
He was caught with Isaac
in the pasture moving sheep,
unarmed, on foot. Outran them,
Isaac couldn't.
They're after horses again
and just killing.
E.K. is getting a posse up. Better
get your people and animals in."

The runner jerked the bay around,
headed north. But by then
Sam was grabbing his gear
and trading the long barrel
for brother Tom's .50 calibre
sharp-shooting needle gun,
and his mother was already
putting on her husband's coat
and hat, thinking about
Tom, thinking about
loading the guns
and setting them up
by the shoot holes
for when the men returned,
or they didn't.
Sam mounted the yellow mare
and headed her for the flats

to find Tom, out there alone,
unarmed, unaware,
driving in the horses
to beat the Texas Norther coming on.

He got to Tom in time to hand him
his gun and get the horses running
for the corral. Then the Indians
struck, screaming and shooting,
splitting the brothers between them.
Sam spurred the mare and two
took after him, the rest chasing
the horses north, ignoring Tom,
frozen in the snarling Christmas snow,
needle gun pointed to heaven,
never firing a shot,
a spectator
sketched against the graying sky,
watching the two closing in
on the seventeenth year of Sam Speer,
shooting him down, dead, on their way
to join the others, rushing
the forty head toward the hills,
too far, too fast, too trailwise
for the Rangers and ranchers
who ran their horses out
before they could issue
the only justice around
and shoot the savages down.

And so the history goes, more or less,
of Sam Speer and his brother Tom—the last man
killed by Indians in Kimble County,
Texas, on a snowy Christmas Eve morning,
1876, and the last witness as well.
They say Tom Speer lost his nerve
and Sebastian Kountz had an unnatural
run of luck because Indians
don't take scalps of black-haired boys.

It could be, though, that settler
and Indian did have one thing in common.
For as Tom held his hammer down
so did two of their kind when they
had poor Sebastian on the ground
point blank, eleven years old,
and wide eyed. What reasons
were forever blown away
by the cold wind that day.
Maybe there comes a moment,
a single frozen moment,
when men have enough of enemies,
on softly snowing days.

The Ghost Dance: August, 1976

"I am the last Indian"
Sitting Bull

Watching the competition dancers at the Dakota Wapici
I think of you, Sitting Bull, and your braves,
dancing rawfooted in the snow
from dawn to dawn in the winter of '90
to fulfill the prophecy of some Nevada Paiute ranch-hand.
All Indians must dance, everywhere, keep on dancing.
Pretty soon in next spring Great Spirit come.
He bring back game of every kind. All dead Indians
come back and live again, be young again. All Indians
go to mountains, high up away from whites. Then
big flood comes and all whites die, get drowned.
After that, water go away and then nobody but Indians
and game all kinds thick. All for a dance, a simple dance.
Did you, the wisest Sioux, believe in Wovoka's Ghost Dance?
Or did you merely bless it, to comfort your people
in their death-dream? No matter:
Bull Head and Red Tomahawk, the Indian policemen,
killed the dream when they killed you.
Because the dancing did not stop, the whites did not know
the dream was dead, the last Indian dead, and so
sprayed their bullets into 300 corpses at Wounded Knee.
And now, 86 years later, while the country celebrates
the 200th year of its Independence,
I watch this Dakota rodeo of song and dance,
looking in all the faces for your face.
But no ghosts dance in their black eyes, no buffalo
stampede in their hearts.
When a little white boy leaves the bleachers
to hop and whoop with the dancers around the sacred tree,
your descendents give him a tom-tom

made of a painted coffee can, then announce
they're on sale near the exit for only $2 plus tax.
This is not their fault. Your death made them ghosts
before their grandparents were born.
And so they too dance a kind of Ghost Dance
but it cannot bring you, or even themselves, back.
Sitting Bull, I thought you should know this.

The White Rose: Sophie Scholl
1921–1943

I

Father, hold my hand.
It is the deep, green and dark forest
where the wild animals spring past
Snow White. Pinecones dot the moss,
and mushrooms, small one-legged people,
stand straight and silent in their scarlet hoods.

Ahead of us a meadow opens
immense, enamelled
with violet, blue, yellow and rose.
I fill my arms with flowers for Mama

and suddenly it is much later,
Inge, Werner, Hans and I
are walking with Father. A cold wind
flattens the grass. I shiver.
Why is Father sad?

"There was once a splendid castle
filled with treasure: carpets
from Isfahan, ruby and cobalt goblets,
rock crystal windows, floors of ebony,
and fountains everywhere. You would have thought
the people who lived there
the luckiest in the world.

"But in the cellar of that castle
a frightful slaughter went on day and night
until blood bubbled up from the ground
and dyed the fountains red."

"But Papa," says Hans, "are you sure,
are you *sure* the Führer knows
about the camps?"

II

A frothy forest of asparagus
gives way to pink and crimson peonies.
I bend until their silken faces
brush mine, their cold, sweet dew
trembles on lips and eyelids.
At the garden's end, a bamboo love-seat—
I open my watercolors, slip into
the skin of the girl
who walks to the edge of the world.

A wooden stool, a water jug and a gold ring
are all she owns. The morning star
lights the way to the glass mountain
but my own knucklebone cut from my finger
unlocks the final door.
"My lords the ravens are abroad . . ."
I drop the ring into the tallest beaker, and now
—and now the flutter of wings—
I am dressed in moonlight, I am wholly hidden
from myself, from Mother's voice—"Sophie?"

III

"Drink your cocoa, Sophie,
you've hardly touched your breakfast."

"Too much to do—the rally this afternoon—
is my blouse ready?"

"And your piano lesson?"
Piano lesson!

"But Mama, the Führer himself is speaking—
you know our troop has to be there.

"Don't *you* want to come?"
She slams the iron down.

"Here—take it—go!"
And then her arms are around me.

"The Pied Piper—remember?"
"Oh Mama—that dumb story—"

IV

I hurry through the arch of yellow roses,
late-blooming petals fluttering like finches
above dark earth embroidered
with strawberries' quaint leaves
and french-knot marigolds.
Gnarled quince trees hung with fragrance
cross-stitch the corners of Frau Seelig's garden.

But where is Rachel?
Where the willow boughs
to weave the little leafy hut
they let me help with?
("Pretend we're in Jerusalem—
it's always summer there, just think,
our walls are branches and our roof-tiles, leaves.")

The neighbor is airing a feather bed
out the window.
"The Seeligs have gone—please leave."
"Gone! But where—"

"Just leave—please! Don't come back."

V

The woods are getting dark—
did I miss the path?
Why didn't Ursel wait for me?
The others
must be far ahead,

I can't hear them singing.
That's because Karla's guitar was smashed
for playing "Alouette."

This is the forest that has no end.
Oak, beech, willow, balsam fir—
a cottage in a clearing,
a village by a ford, a smithy.
Trails fork and join and run to bramble,
past bogs and mountains, traveled
by mandrake gatherers, peddlers, gypsies
—and now me.

Already it's swallowed up
the other Germany, the one
I've lost my way in.
Are there wild animals? The raven
brings me ripe blackberries, wolf, boar and stag
will never harm me:
I'm the chameleon salamander
that nests in fire.

How still the trees are.
Not a breath of wind,
just these great level shafts
of evening light
as though a door's about to open . . .

VI
They're calling it *Kristallnacht*—lovely word
that makes you think of jewelled chandeliers'
blaze in a midnight-blue and silver ballroom
where waltzing couples whirl, and violins
set all the drops of moonlight trembling.
                                    Night
of smashed and trampled lives,
the image in the mirror crazed and blinded
beyond repair. Oh delicate splinters, stars

sparkling like tears on the soiled face of earth,
oh piercing, bloody fragments: Crystal.
                                        Night.

VII
—the sound we wait for. Wail
rising and falling in my sleep   shocked
torn awake   stumble
into clothes
I grab Inge's hand   *quick hurry*
Father at the cellar door
It's all right—don't rush
Werner, here's the thermos. Hans
your coat   rising, falling
Where's Mother—here, Sophie
take this blanket.   CRASH and
CRASH   rattle of anti-aircraft
let it hit somewhere else   please God
CRASH   not this house   not us
walls tremble, tinkle of glass   CRASH   fainter
this time   thank God further   silence
the All Clear.

In the morning   school   a heap
I don't understand   but where
of rubble.

VIII
                        You said
                "He is a scourge of God"—
                    this is for you, Father,
                in prison: our great beech
            at sunset, bole of light, each leaf
            viridian flame, crown of branches
                shivering light into the wind.
        And this—white sail on azure, blending
        to deepest ultramarine, blue of the infinite
                    to set you free.
            When you look at these paintings,
                    think of me.

IX

Am I the only one awake?
Moonlight pours through the windows,
I could almost read my forbidden book of poems.

My muscles ache, but that's nothing.
I could like this student work-camp, mindless hours
on top of the haystack, heaping up

sweet-smelling meadowgrass, sunlight and sweat
in my eyes, Ursel below me laughing,
her thick braids stuck with burrs.

"For the Führer!" she cries, and tosses me
a gold-green forkful—
"for victory!"

I think of Werner at the Eastern front,
of Father in jail, I think of Father's words
"We have no choice but hope for our defeat." I try

not to salute the flag,
not to give the Hitler-greeting,
to be invisible.

Some days we're let off early.
I duck along the hedge-rows till I reach
the church beyond the flax fields.

My book, hidden under a fallen gravestone
waits for me, the creaky organ
groans and booms beneath my hands.

Sometimes I lie in the churchyard watching the clouds.
The war seems far away. How will it be
when my life finally starts?

X

"Beloved, let us pray
also for Yakov Androvenko,
forced-laborer in this parish
who was beaten to death—"
in the night, Herr Pastor Harms
is arrested
—but our whole country is a prison.
A friend of Hans's returned from the front
to find his wife—an epileptic,
pregnant with their first child—
gassed.

Today in a shuffling, close-packed column
of old men, women, young girls and boys
all wearing yellow stars
all carrying suitcases,
I saw a baby playing peek-a-boo
over his mother's shoulder. His laughter
spurted into the smoky air
like jets of blood.

XI

Green and purple stormclouds heaped
above the stifling house, mutter
of thunder, quick tattoo
of raindops:
I rush to the roof
where laundry billows, grab flapping armfuls
of sheets, towels, tablecloths.
Little Franzi Schmid is with me.

Lightning cracks the sky—blanched skeletons
of trees, bolt on bolt
of thunder—Franzi grabs my skirt,
I fold my arms around him.
"It's all right," I tell him, "look,
this lightning rod will draw the fire
safely to earth."

The child shivers.
"And does God know about the lightning rod?"
"This one and all the others.
If He didn't
there wouldn't be one stone left on another
in all the world."

XII

Munich seems vast to me
coming from little Ulm. And everywhere the grisly
bombed buildings, gaping like smashed dollhouses
—you can see where stairs went up, tatters
of flowered wallpaper, a picture hanging crazily
above charred heaps that once were chairs.

Strange, how in the midst of this
we can still laugh together,
still celebrate.
Father's release, my first day
at the University—
Hans and his friends gave a party for me.
Mother sent plum cake—a month's rations—
we trailed a bottle of wine, by moonlight,
in the chill River Isar
and Alex played his balalaika, gypsy love songs,
their dark, harsh chords, their
foreign harmonies.

Later we talked. And Hans: "It sickens me—
the irony of medical school, healing people
for Hitler to feed into this roaring furnace
of war—and into those—into those other ovens. . . ."
I can't remember who first spoke the word
resistance. Then Christoph—
"How can we hold our heads up ever again,
a nation of cowards ruled by criminals?"

What if we win this war? Already
they are warning us
that rather than hang around the universities
we should be "making a child for Hitler."
My flesh creeps—I want to plunge into my studies
as into a cleansing stream.

XIII
In large, clear letters on the blackboard
Professor Huber's text from Lao Tzu:

*Do you think you can take over the universe
and improve it?
If you try to hold it you will lose it.*

*If you rejoice in victory
you delight in killing.
Force is followed by loss of strength.*

*That which goes against the Tao
comes to an early end.*

The mild words are an open dare.
If just one student should denounce him?
Watching him balance on that knife-edge
I draw deep breaths of icy mountain air.

XIV
Leaflets on floors and windowsills
—with pounding heart I read
*Nothing is so unworthy of a civilized nation
as that it should permit itself to be governed
by an irresponsible ruling caste
that has surrendered
to its darkest instincts . . .
resist . . . a people deserves that government
it tolerates . . . resist . . .*

We're not alone, then—
there are others like us!
In the main lecture hall
Women with pails and brushes
are scrubbing slogans off the walls:
DOWN WITH HITLER!
FREEDOM!

Goosebumps along my arms
—it's in the air,
spark of resistance—flame—fire—

In classes, whispering excitement.
Impossible to keep my mind
on philosophy today.
I rush to Hans's room
—he'll have spent the morning at the lab
and won't have seen the flyers.
A book lies open on his desk,
a sentence, lightly underlined
leaps out: *a people deserves*
that government it tolerates.

O merciful God.

XV
Why must it be me?
  Why not you?
But there are others, political people—
  The work is not political.
people who understand this kind of thing—
  What don't you understand?
organizations—
  We are born and die alone.
I don't want to die.
  The work is urgent.
Oh please, please don't
  The decision is yours.
I'm so afraid.
  Yes.

XVI

Breathless, in the streetcar. Beside me
an S.S. officer fidgets, glances restlessly
about. Once, horribly,
I catch his eye. My briefcase
burns into my side, I can't stop
seeing the clasp give way, papers
spilling, whirling into people's laps—
does it look odd? Too full?
Should I have looked away so quickly?

The ticket collector—
breathe deeply—don't run—I fumble
with change—the briefcase
slips, crashes down, the officer
grabs it   his face swims before my eyes
—hands it back, smiling—
hot trickle of terror down my leg

There are times at night
when I *am* fear, icy, my bones
liquid, blood humming in darkness
listening. I pray to sleep, I pray
to wake and find myself and Hans,
Christoph and Alex and the others
just students again.
The deadly pressure lifted.

XVII

I had forgotten
pines and clouds and mountains:
sketching with Alex
on this sunny hillside,
a yellow daisy in my hair.

A kestrel spirals in the air below us.
Honeybees murmur in the briar roses,
and at our backs is a warm tangle
of roots and boulders.

We feed crumbs of ersatz cheese
to a fat meadow mouse
that sits, absurd, on Alex's shoe
and combs its whiskers.

How temporary the gray dollhouses,
the toy train puffing through quilted fields
are, after all. Smudges
on earth's green pelt.

XVIII

My eyes are gritty—Professor Huber and I
up all night with the ditto machine
and two air raids which we ignore.

At four, Hans, Alex, Christoph and Willi
in high spirits,
dripping red paint:

"Wait till you see the Ludwigsstrasse
—and it's peacetime paint,
they won't get that off in a hurry!"

I'm wide awake now. Alex:
"Let's celebrate!" Christoph has goat cheese
his wife sent from their mountain village,

Hans brings a bottle of Riesling
he's been saving, Willi cigarettes
and Alex his zany songs and Hitler-jokes,

and for an hour or two
we forget the work, the world
—how long since I last laughed out loud?

Herr Huber looks years younger, Hans relaxed,
the deep line gone between his eyes, and Alex
—but Alex never seems to lose his sparkle.

When Christoph says "look—sunrise"
exhaustion overwhelms me. My eyes close,
soft notes of the balalaika . . . sinking . . .

XIX
Today another one of those strange
messages I have been getting lately.
A warning? A coincidence?
We've talked of flight—

Yesterday morning
a cleaning woman came out of a doorway,
began to sweep the leaflets from the stoop.
I forced out words—my mouth dry flannel—
"Please leave those papers, they're
for people to read."
She looked at me with blank hostility.
"No understand"—a Polish prisoner.

Will I ever paint again?
I only feel alive, now,
when I'm about our work
—my senses taut until I vibrate,
my whole body
tuned to a voice, a footfall.
Each letter from home
cuts like a knife—I would give anything
to turn,
pick up my books, my paintbrush,
my life.

XX
Some people believe
this is the end of the world.

But isn't death the same
no matter what age you live in?

I could be killed
by accident, a bomb

—would I bear less responsibility
for my life

if I went down together
with earth and stars?

XXI

It is morning, the University
about to open. In the stillness
before voices, the slam and clatter
of doors, our footsteps
sound like shots. Hans and I
lean over the topmost bannister, empty
our bags. A snowfall of paper
settles on landings, stairs.
                              Relief,
familiar, welling nausea.
I grasp the railing
to keep my legs from giving way.
Hans hugs me, our eyes meet. His
are glowing. "Let's get out of here."

We take the stairs two at a time,
reach the door, which
and time slows
stops   won't open   impossible
won't

          open
                    I'm still trying
to grasp   why is the janitor   sirens
"Hans! the police"
uniformed men surround us

so quickly done

XXII

Stripped naked, my chain with the gold cross
broken, clothes
turned inside out, seams slit, flesh

shrinking from hard fingers
when very quietly,
"If you have anything forbidden on you
destroy it now. I'm a prisoner too."

A trap? I almost think
if I think hard enough
I could get back and wrench that door open
the trapdoor we fell through.
I'm still falling.
The world is slipping, speeding past
and I am light, lighter than breath
falling or floating
between life and death.

The clothes she gives me hang on me
as though already
my body takes up less space.

XXIII

An entire day and night
of questioning—light-headed—
a kind of game
—so far I think
I've managed not to give
one name they don't yet have.
Alex? Please God . . .

The officers who question me
seem puzzled.
I was even offered coffee.
"If you had realized, Fräulein Scholl,
how you have undermined the war effort,
surely you would have acted differently?"

Christoph, Herr Huber, Willi, Alex—my mind
shuts around you—not one crack of light
—silence
        the room
            tilts

I am given a hurried meal of soup and bread
before I am taken back upstairs.
My cell-mate, entering, has just time
to whisper to me they have pulled in Christoph.

Hans, you're the rock I grasp
though they don't let me see you
I hear your voice
—your voice beneath their voices—
in my head.

Do you hear mine?

Christoph.
Let them not murder Christoph.

This paper and pencil
—I am to write out
a full confession with
names and dates—was there a hint
it could save me?

Sleep . . . I lay me down to sleep
I pray

XXIV

It is night. The Isar
gleams and sparkles where the moon
weaves a silver web across the water.

I am sitting on the bank
among forget-me-nots
and I am knitting—

knitting a shirt—but not with wool,
with nettles.
They sting my fingers.

Is the moon
fainter now, the night more gray?
I have to finish

before dawn. I gaze
at the deep, swirling water—
a swan floats past,

his wings are raised,
the dark and human eyes
are fixed on me.

I have to throw the stinging shirt
across his wings,
his black, webbed feet

and break the spell.
The shirt is almost done,
just one sleeve left to finish—

but my cold fingers
won't move, my hands
lie lifeless in my lap—

wings beating like my heart
—wake, love, the dawn—
but you are weeping . . .

XXV
Mother, I think of you,
blank horror on your face, hearing
what you must know by now—
my tears
uncontrollably fall and fall

Hush, don't, don't *you* cry.

Remember the dead child
who in the story comes to his grieving mother
and wrings her tears out of his winding-sheet

and begs her to stop weeping
and begs her
to let him lie still and peaceful
in his grave

We'll cry this once together
and then
no more.

XXVI
The indictment—so thick
the list of all my crimes?

In spite of myself
my hands
shake
I can hardly hold it
much less read
the type that
blurs
and
chatters on the page.
I force myself
to look
to look
until the words stand
clear
black and implacable:
High Treason.

XXVII
Breathe
deeply—my fingers dig into the mattress
—only three days ago
years lay spread out before me.

Does anyone know
how soft my brown hair was,
how warm my skin?

No man has seen me naked.
                              No lover
will ever cup my breasts in his hands.

—A kind of sleep? I've never been
so wide awake.
My skull is a clear airless glass
—words flutter
                    and drop   how fast
the minutes are creeping by
this ringing in my ears
                              Hans
are you icy cold as I am
will it hurt to die

XXVIII

Without warning, and against
all reason
I am drowned and flooded
with joy at being alive,
and I am glad, yes *glad*
and would not change one moment
of what has happened.

Like a spell
like a prayer my mind repeats
Rilke's great poem

O tell us, poet, what is it you do?
—I praise.

But in the midst of deadly turmoil, what
helps you to endure and how do you survive?
—I praise.

I tell my court-appointed lawyer
Hans has the right to die
before a firing squad, having been a medic
at the front.

When I ask
if I am to be hanged or beheaded
his pen jerks in his hand,
his eyes slide past me. "But Fräulein Scholl,
there is still hope."

XXIX
Hans—dearest brother and friend—
will we speak to each other again?
You were to have been a great physician.

Oh believe—we must believe—already
in all our cities—
Hamburg, Köln, Berlin,

at all the universities, a wave
of resistance is breaking like the dawn
over Germany.

So many thousands of people can't be silenced
though they silence us.

This is to say goodbye.

XXX
What a jagged gap it leaves—
the future.

Every solid thing's
a kind of light
that flashes in and out of now.

The chaplain speaks of Heaven
as though it were a place.

Sometimes I hear
how the whole world
—trees, oceans, stars and animals—
is saying *I am*

just as my inmost self
repeats—oh without end—

How could there ever not be
that *I am*, how could there not be
God?

XXXI
A mild, blue February day.
Everything yearns toward spring, outside
primroses are opening. Sun
spills like yellow pollen
through my barred window.

Light burned all night in my cell.
I dreamed
I carried a baby to its christening.
The way to the church lay over fields.
Suddenly the ground
opened at my feet—
I had just time to throw the child to safety
before—before I
woke.

I have written everyone in the family,
having been warned
that after the trial there will be
no time.

XXXII
Judge Freisler himself
was flown here for our trial.
Blood-red robes, cold heavy-lidded eyes
—so everything has been decided.

Hans. After these dark days and nights—your smile, warm
sunshine. Christoph's blue, blue eyes.
Out there, a blur—so many people?
Mother and Father, I am willing you
to come   dear God to come in time

"Traitors, sniveling trash—"
Freisler actually foams at the mouth, rage
shakes him like a terrier a rat

it has nothing to do with me.

Silence—a question—
I shake my head, no. Hans
is saying something

Freisler's mouth
a black hole dribbling . . . *treason*

to be beheaded. Beheaded.
Beheaded.

XXXIII

      A still and luminous room.
      Mother and Father—it is only air
      that parts us, not this silly barrier.
      I hardly feel the floor beneath my feet.

—We've brought—they let us bring—
this chocolate—Hans
didn't want any—

                 —Will they arrest you, too?
—We're in God's hands
as you are, Sophie—

I've never seen you
so beautiful—but you're trembling—
                 —I'm not afraid.
                 Mama? I promise
                 I'm not afraid.

XXXIV

No light shines
but a sun is in my eyes
and everything that ever was, is now.
A rhythm where we change, part
come together
and part again in one unbroken flow.
And I am running in a mountain meadow
"I'll never see you any more"
wind lifts my hair, and though my forehead
touches hard wood
my arms are full of flowers
gentian, primrose, daisy, as cloud-shadows
race across the grass. "And, Sophie . . . Jesus?"
And now the music brings us back together
Christoph, Hans and me
"I never knew that it could be so easy"
a crimson blossom opens without sound
we are this rhythm
I let go your hand

NOTE: This poem is based on the true story of the student resistance movement organized by Hans and Sophie Scholl in 1941. They called their group the White Rose. Professor Kurt Huber, Willi Graf and Alexander Schmorell were also subsequently caught and executed.

Tending the Garden

A prisoner-of-war graveyard outside the
disciplinary camp of Brodno in Volynia

1.

The clod of earth in his shovel
was a familiar weight
he had lifted and set aside all day.
By noon, his hands were a dull orange of rust.
If in the wood's damp shadow
white smoke lifted through the branches,
he did not see it, nor did he hear
the whistle yet, releasing steam—its sound
trailing behind the train, the train moving
toward him and the other prisoners
—some digging graves, some planting flowers.
All he knew of death was its weight
as he lowered the bodies by worn ropes
to the moist soil dark with leafmold.
He knew each day there would be new dead.
It did not matter. It was a matter of waiting:
typhus, pneumonia, a frail body limp
in the barbed fence.

He leaned on his shovel and listened
to the train's slow jolting
as it emerged from the trees.
He knew he could dig all day
and it would be useless—only a hole, not a tunnel. . . .
At a certain depth he would climb out
and begin again. There was no other end.
It was best to have a few dug in advance.
Canvas could be stretched over to keep the rain out
and boards placed against the walls
to keep the sides from tumbling in.

As the sun came out from the thick clouds,
a raw gleam of light fell
on the boxcars, then alternate slants of shadow.
He knew what freight the train carried—
white faces framed by narrow slats.

2.

I was luckier than most, luckier
because I don't remember the pain
if there was pain—only the oddity
of tending a graveyard and flowerbeds;
how we convinced the Germans to give us
the materials to build a white fence—
a small luxury for our unnamed dead
and for ourselves. It was our livelihood
to find enough work to last the whole day
before we would have to go back to camp,
back to the dirty barracks where we slept.
The other prisoners were envious
of our duty. It was, at times, hard work,
but the work, it seems, promoted our health.
I was determined to stay well, to last
through the coming winter and not end up
face up in a grave my own hands had dug.

Ernst, the eldest guard, chose to befriend me
and offered me hot tea and cigarettes.
He spoke French as poorly as I spoke German.
He said he was Catholic and we shared that
at least. And though I was not Catholic,
his believing it was a thing to share.
He did not understand the war, but joined
because there was little work, and his wife
had left him earlier that year. He thought
she had joined a circus. One had passed through
town the same week she decided to leave.
It was a story he liked to believe.

I thought I loved a woman then. A girl.
I met her only once. She walked the road
below the graveyard before noon, two pails
of water in her hands, a white armlet
on her sleeve. I believe her name was Sarah.
She must be dead by now. She might have died
shortly after the last day I saw her.
They were collecting Jews near Brodno then.
On her armlet was the Star of David.
I might have kissed her that day by the road
but I did not. Ernst wouldn't have cared.
But now, nothing as obvious as a kiss
could reinvent that girl or change anything.

3.
That night he woke on the wooden bunk
and his feet were cold, his neck stiff.
They were given no straw to sleep on
for fear of propagating lice.
Above him, a Russian prisoner laughed in his sleep.
At times the laughter caught in his throat
and it sounded like a man choking.
He tried not to look too closely at the ill.

That night he dreamed winter had come and passed.
The rain and thaw washed away the unpaved streets
and duckboards were thrown down
to let the soldiers pass.
A line of villagers stood motionless,
the muddy water around their ankles,
their armlets gray in rain.
The train was delayed. . . .

That night he woke on the wooden bunk
and realized if despair can be held,
it has the weight of a tuft of earth
and is bitter held close to the face.
It is what might cover one and take one's breath away,
completely, a final time.

4.

The trains pass more frequently. The whistle
is blown less as if to avoid notice.
Sometimes I hear the train in the forest
and I stop shoveling. Do they watch
as I watch them?—a digger of graves
surrounded by shrubs, wood-sorrel, weeds.
Is their murmuring I can't hear prayer?
I cannot imagine their journey
or what they might say to one another
if anything, how the pain in their legs
must grow. Beneath the faces in the slats
a child might hold its mother's legs.
I hear only the sound of the train
and Ernst's coughing and the thud of earth
tossed up in piles beside the new grave.
Once in France, before the war, I rode
all day on a crowded train to Paris.
And at one stop a gang of boys
boarded, cussed loudly and drank wine.
As we departed, one boy calmly spat
on his window making the others laugh.
Beside me, an old woman shook her head
and said in all her years she had not seen
anything so awful. It seems odd now
that it mattered to her and not me,
and that I would choose to remember it
on this particular day, this moment.

5.

She thought it was unusual
when the prisoner started walking toward her
down the hill below the graveyard.
And for a moment she thought he was escaping,
but his stride was casual, slow.
His blond hair was cut short like a boy's.
She smiled at him as he tripped
crossing the ditchbank.
The water grew heavy in her pails,

but she did not think of lowering them.
One guard walked along the embankment
then sat down in the unmown grass.
As she spoke her name
she heard the other prisoners talking
as they worked—their words
seemed almost recognizable until she listened.
She had spent so much time learning not to listen,
not to hear the few gunshots at night,
or her mother in the next room
with the pocked-faced corporal from the motor pool
who swore he'd kill them both if they told anyone.
Her mother liked it.
Or else she wouldn't make those noises,
make herself sound like a pig.
Once she went out at night after stealing
the corporal's watch and buried it in a tin
among the rocks and red mud of the creekbed.
The crystal was chipped and the inscription,
in a language she did not know, was worn.
Sometimes she would wake and watch
the patrol walking outside her window
and hear the soldiers laugh loudly.
Sometimes she watched their faces lit
by the flare of a single match,
the way, now, the sun gave exact angles
to the prisoner's features.
He said very little. Hello. Asked her name.
He held out a clump of morning glories
he had found at the wood's shaded edge.
She lifted the pails slightly at her sides
to show she could not accept the gift.

6.
The man beside her cried.
But his cries were not
distinguishable from the others',
or from her own breathing,
or from the train.

She could not know
that by the second day
the man beside her would die
or that the infant
in the young woman's arms
had been dead all along,
but the woman would not let go,
that whatever prayers she said
would only consume
the boxcar's thin air.
The stronger passengers
pressed toward the slats.
She watched as lines of light
revealed the faces in the car.
She could not know
that later in the week
when she breathed the gas,
it would burn her throat
and when the women around her
collapsed on the shower floor,
she would remain standing
for one moment, as if balancing,
the way she would balance
on the fallen logs as she walked home,
the two pails as counterweights,
and when she did fall
she would feel the floor
cold against her shoulders.
She could not know
that when her train passed
the prisoner looked up,
blocking the sun from his eyes,
but did not catch any one face in the slats.
He rested on his shovel
and began to dig again.
She could at times catch glimpses
of trees and the men
working along the roadside.
She could not know

that when her clothes were taken
to be deloused
she would be ashamed of her body,
its whiteness startling
in the cool light of afternoon,
and she would cover her new breasts
and the dark patch of hair
with her hands and arms
and realize she would never touch
herself as intimately
or with such a pure and generous fear.

7.
I often think of going back.
Curiosity. To see what's left there,
to see how the years have let the earth grow wild,
how the ferns and thistle have replaced
the small garden of flowers we planted.

Ernst was shot. Did I mention that before?
Desertion or looting. I can't remember.
Maybe he was trying to find his wife.
No. He wouldn't have died for her sake—
Maybe I was never told the right story.

I try not to think about it much,
but sometimes I think of being buried alive.
Everyone must have those thoughts, though.
I think one night a runaway Jew hid
in an empty grave I had dug.

In the morning I found nutshells, some crumbs
of bread, the impression of a body
on the soaked black earth. I hope
he survived, if he ever existed. . . .

The Madhouse

I cannot give you the squeak
of the blue chalk on the cue tip,
the sound of the break, or the movement
about the table, like a ritual of wine;

then I was not born. My father,
who saw it, was still in high school;
and there are others who remember
the poolroom on the avenue.

Here lounged the former heroes
of the high-school team, who took
the Tri-State Crown in '24, and tied
with Massillon in '25. Catholics all,

a backfield composed of Swede
Svendson at fullback, the Baxter brothers
at either half, and handsome Richard
O'Reilly at the quarter.

They had no peers, then or now.
On Saturdays regularly they stood,
hats firmly on their heads, watching
the procession of hooded Klansmen

coming up Anderson Street, heading
toward the Main intersection. Always
the Klan demanded hats removed
before the flag they carried,

always the boys at the Madhouse refused,
and began unscrewing the weighted ends
of their pool cues. People came to watch;
the police stood apart; the Klan

never got past the Madhouse. That
was years ago. They're all dead now,
Swede and the Baxter boys, and
handsome Richard O'Reilly,

who married the banker's daughter;
and the Klansmen too. Only the men
who were boys then can still remember.
They talk about it, even now,

sitting in Joe's barbershop
watching cars go by, or sipping a beer
in Condon's tavern. It is a story
I heard when I was a boy. Lately

there's been a doughnut shop
where the Madhouse used to stand.
Mornings when I stop for coffee
I can almost hear it: the nine ball

dropping in the corner pocket,
the twelve rolling to within an inch
of the side; voices in the street
echoing along the store fronts.

Progress

I reckon it was in the early Fifties
when they finally got the electric up at Smith.
I was hired to go behind the linemen
selling stoves, washers, Frigidaires.

Well, anyway, there was this one woman
I saw as I came around a bend
with her washtub set up beneath a poplar
singing like a bird at first light.

She seemed awful glad to see me,
took my hand in her soapy hand
but it wasn't any washer that she wanted.
No sir, she wanted a hi-fi.

Paid cash—a hundred and some dollars—
set the hi-fi right on the dirt floor.
Full blast, Nashville filled the holler
and saved her all the drudgery of song.

The New Lady Barber
at Ralph's Barber Shop

She's in there all right,
cutting hair alongside Ralph.
From California, they say,
young, blond, and built.
A woman has no business
being a barber, we said.
But soon we saw
how Old Man Brunner walked
back and forth
past the barber shop,
not going in until
someone was in Ralph's chair
and hers was empty.
In a month we were all
glancing into Ralph's window,
timing our haircuts.
A woman has no business
being a barber, our wives say.
One thing is dead certain
in this town:
we will never have topless
dancers or massage parlors.
When strangers ask
what we do for excitement,
we can say we got a lady barber
if your timing is right.

Remodeling the Hermit's Cabin

Not what we expected. And dark in there,
The one little window not precisely a window
But a chopped-out off-square page of cloud and treetop
That let a grayness in. No pin-up girls
Leggy in froth panties, but recipes
On the walls, head-heavy crayons of hawks,
Torn-out leaves of Bibles, pictures of flowers.
"This old feller was a different kind of lonesome,"
Reade said. We didn't understand. The bed
Was rusty and narrow. The floor was bare.

We found his handiwork. A carved and sanded
Walking stick with a twice-twined rattlesnake
Leaned in the corner. Ferrule and knob smeared silvery,
The snake was blotched unlikely black and orange.
Reade hefted it for balance. "I've seen worse,"
He said. "This old-time whittling, you always wonder
Where they got the hours. I've started I guess
A dozen, and never finished one worth carrying."
In a corner shelf we found his Little People,
Whittled men and women and children hand-sized,
Naked, or dressed in closely twisted cornshuck,
Disposed in attitudes forlorn and studied,
Each inhabiting a single space
That set it well apart from all the others,
Even in the narrow shelf. "His family,
How he remembers the way it was," Reade said.
"You see they didn't get along too good,
But what the story is would be a puzzle.
This one here is him." The only doll
He didn't give a face, an oval of soft
White pink blank as a thumbnail, a spindly figure
Turned toward the ragged chinked log wall, unclothed,

And set apart from the drama the other dolls
Absorbed themselves in, deaf or contemptuous
Of passions fierce for all their littleness,
Fiercer perhaps because of littleness—
A figure the world had cut no features on,
Musing the Godlike wall that was his mirror.

We swept them all into a cardboard box.

Outside, we gathered our courage. "That Florida buyer
Wants us to raise the roof," Reade said, "and lower
The floor. Might be we'll do the roof pretty easy,
Just loosen the nails and shim it up with blocks
Wedged in under the joists. But would you look
At them foundation beams? That main one there
Must be two-and-a-half foot square, and dug in
Solid where it's set a hundred years."
"Whose cabin was it before the hermit came?"
"Old hunting club from the turn of the century.
Before that, I don't know. Daniel Boone's,
I reckon. Don't see logs like that no more."
He measured it with his tape. "What'd I tell you?
Thirty inches, and lodged into the hill
Since the flood of Noah." "Well, what are we going to do?"
"Rassle it," he said, "unless you've got
A better notion."
                    We wrestled it. And broke
The handles of two twelve-pound sledges, and bent
His faithful old black crowbar into a U,
We stopped for a cup of water from the S-
Shaped runlet below the spring. "Takes a grade-A
Fool to take this ruction job," Reade said.
"They could have paid us to cut a window or two
And left it like it was. There ain't no way
We'll get the foundation as stout as it used to be."
"What do you reckon it cost to build this cabin?"
"Twenty-eight dollars and twelve and one-half cents,
In pure cash money. Then you've got your labor,
And the time it took to think the construction out,

And whatever it's worth to stand out independent
And be thought lunatic or just plain dumb."
"It looks kind of sad and busted, what we've done,"
I said.
   "That Florida feller will tack some plastic
Around," he said, "and put in an ice-cube maker,
And have him a sliding-door carport and a poodle
He's trained to count his money. These modern days
We're all a bunch of cowbirds, you know that?"

To Raise a Chimney

I climbed down to the stream and looked back
past landslide and fallen logs to the house
and the impossible distances
where the chimney would be. Braced
against the current and the slippery bank
I lifted stone after stone
to the sound of a long, wet kiss
as the water released them.
Piled under a bay tree they sparkled and dripped,
veins of quartz glistening in the granite.
One by one I carried them up the hill.
To catch my breath I sang out loud,
hymns recalled from childhood,
as if that, too, had been a difficult labor.
Such odd strength in that cadence.
I kept its rhythm and mixed mortar
the consistency of dough. The stones
were laid down. I felt the warmth
of the mortar as it cured and set.
I climbed the scaffold, placed more stones
and the chimney rose. It rose
and the air below was drawn up and exhaled
in one unending breath. It rose and began
to moan as if the ground
had discovered a mouth to bellow through.
Looking down from that height
I had no fear of falling. I was afraid
of climbing forever, singing hymns like an angel
and moving stone by stone away from the earth.

Moving

The house inside still looks like a house
but the blank rectangle of light
through the propped-open front door
means emptiness. Inside, the slow men
move like mourners, non-committal
among the labeled furniture, once decent
but today grown strangely shabby. Each table
is listed "scratched." In brightening
room to room, our pine-planked voices echo
as if they never spoke here before.

We watch moments of our lives move out
piece by piece through the front door
carelessly handled with care
by, for the moment, members of the family.
(Moving out, they move in,
helplessly intimate, their big arms
touching our things, hauling
the weight of what we are.)
We feel apologetic to be so heavy
and stand around like guests being served
saying, "Yes, that," and, "No, not that,"
watching decor become debris, and sunlight
sanding the floors already.

The Courtship

When Sickly Jim Wilson's first wife died
he tried to carry on
keep house and farm his scrabbly land
and it like to broke him.
All them kids were too old to stay put
and too young to carry water. There was no one
to cook, wash, or sew, no one but Sickly Jim
and him the same body who must milk the cow
and plant the scanty hay. Soon he saw
he had to have another wife.

He considered the prospects on the creek,
listed them according to his favor:
Widow Jones, Miss Creech, the oldest Phillips girl,
and even Mossie Maggern. The thought of Mossie
made his belly cold, but next morning he set out.

Widow Jones was stringing beans on her hillside
porch. He rode right up to the rail.
"Morning Miz Jones. How are you now?"
"Working steady," was her answer,
"and how about yourself?" "Not faring well,
not faring well at all. If I'm to farm
and raise my kids, I've got to have a helpmeet.
That's why I'm here. It looks to me
like you might be the one. What do you say?"

She studied him, walked to the edge of the porch.
"I didn't think wives were got
the way a man gets pigs or harness.
I thought it usually took a little time
and a feller got off his horse."
"You know, Miz Jones, I mean no offense
but time's a thing I've run short of.

I've got babies crying at home
and so I speak out plain."
"Well give me the day. You come back
around suppertime for my answer."
"No ma'am. I need a wife before that."
He looked at the paper in his hand.
"You're the first on my list, but if you
can't oblige, I'll be off to try Miss Creech."

He settled his hat, turned his horse,
and was almost out of the yard
when she called to him, "I've given it thought.
It's clear I'm the wife you need.
Hold till Sunday and I'll marry you."
And that's just what she did.

Mountain Bride

They say Revis found a flatrock
on the ridge just
perfect for a natural hearth,
and built his cabin with a stick

and clay chimney right over it.
On their wedding night he lit
the fireplace to dry away the mountain
chill of late spring, and flung on

applewood to dye
the room with molten color while
he and Martha that was a Parrish
warmed the sheets between the tick

stuffed with leaves and its feather
cover. Under that wide hearth
a nest of rattlers,
they'll knot a hundred together,

had wintered and were coming awake.
The warming rock
flushed them out early.
It was she

who wakened to their singing near
the embers and roused him to go look.
Before he reached the fire
more than a dozen struck

and he died yelling her to stay
on the big four-poster.
Her uncle coming up the hollow
with a gift bearham two days later

found her shivering there
marooned above a pool
of hungry snakes,
and the body beginning to swell.

Lester Tells of Wanda and
the Big Snow

Some years back I worked a strip mine
Out near Tylersburg. One day it starts
To snow and by two we got three feet.
I says to the foreman, "I'm going home."
He says, "Ain't you staying till five?"
I says, "I got to see to my cows,"
Not telling how Wanda was there at the house.
By the time I make it home at four
Another foot is down and it don't quit
Until it lays another. Wanda and me
For three whole days seen no one else.
We tunneled the drifts, we slid
Right over the barbed wire and laughed
At how our heartbeats melted the snow.
After a time the food was gone and I thought
I would butcher a cow, but then it cleared
And the moon come up as sweet as an apple.
Next morning the ploughs got through. It made us sad.
It don't snow like that no more. Too bad.

Jill, Afterwards

He had this idea about the hill,
How at the top there would be water
Sweeter than any in any pail
Lugged previously, and to come down
Would be the easiest part of all.
I told him it was a kids' story.

Before I had knockers that story
Was making the rounds in my gang. Hell,
We laughed at it even then. We all
Knew better than to think sweet water
Could be had for the price of a pail
And a little leg-work up and down

A hill that had been standing there, dawn
To dreary dawn, our whole life's story
Long. Not to mention the probabil-
ity such a thing as sweet water,
Hill or no hill, didn't exist. I'll
Give him credit for this, though: a wall

Couldn't have been more stubborn. He'd call
Me late at night even, to break down
My resistance. Okay, I said, I'll
Go. The truth is, he was cute. Starry-
eyed, but cute. And I wondered whether
He had anything in his pants. Pale

Dawn found us taking turns with the pail
As we rose above the town. Not all
The money down there beats the water
We'll find, he said. Now I was poor, down
To a few bucks. It's no mystery
Money talks. Loud. But I climbed the hill.

To the top. And there was this big hole.
And deep. I got dizzy to look down
It. He had rope and let the pail fall
Yards and yards. "Got something," he yelled, pull-
ing the catch in. Later, the story
He told, back in town, was the water

Spilled out. But the fact of the matter
Is I saw what he had. Nothing. Damn
If he didn't claim different, though. Al-
ways. Damn, too, if his pants weren't full.
I've got these kids to prove that story.
When they whine, I tell them: climb a hill.

At the Piano

One night two hunters, drunk, came in the tent.
They fired their guns and stood there stupidly
as Daddy left the pulpit, stalked toward them,
and slapped them each across the mouth. He split
one's upper lip.
               They beat him like a dog.
They propped their guns against the center pole,
rolled up their sleeves as Daddy stood and preached
about the desecration of God's house.
They punched him down, took turns kicking his ribs,
while thirty old women and sixteen men
sat slack-jawed in their folding chairs and watched.
Just twelve, not knowing what to do, I launched
into "Amazing Grace"—the only hymn
I knew by heart—and everybody sang.
We sang until the hunters grew ashamed
—or maybe tired—and left, taking their guns,
their faces red and gleaming from the work.

They got three years suspended sentence each
and Daddy got another tale of how
Christians are saints and strangers in the world.
I guess he knows. He said that I'd done right
to play the song. God's music saved his life.
But I don't know. I couldn't make a guess.
Can you imagine what it means to be
just barely twelve, a Christian and a girl,
and see your father beaten to a pulp?
Neither can I, God knows, and I was there
in the hot tent, beneath the mildewed cloth,
breathing the August, Alabama air,
and I don't know what happened there, to me.
I told this to my second husband, Jim.

We were just dating then. I cried a lot.
He said, *Hush, dear, at least your father got
a chance to turn all four of his cheeks.*
I laughed. I knew, right then, I was in love.
But still I see that image of my father,
his weight humped on his shoulders as he tried
to stand, and I kept plunging through the song
so I could watch my hands and not his face,
which was rouged crimson with red clay and blood.

The Gift

When I was five my father kidnapped me.
He didn't keep me long enough to worry
My mother. She may not have even known.
But I knew, even five years old. That day
At school he stood at the big double doors
And beyond him was his shiny new Hudson.
I knew he'd come when he was not supposed to.
He said it was all right, my mother knew.
There was a gift for me on the front seat
That he said to unwrap as the car started.
But the ribbon snarled and the gift box buckled.
He was driving. He couldn't stop to help.
Outside the windshield traffic lights hung down
From cables, and the bushy tops of palms
Appeared at intervals that I could count.
A pink or yellow building front skimmed past.
But mostly I could only see the sky.
(My window was set high above my shoulder.
A child could hardly see from those old cars.)
The sky went by, pale blue and white and empty,
Crossed suddenly by wire. And I gave up
Trying to take the wrapping off my present
Until we reached wherever we were going.
Then, at a stop, one of those tall palm trees
That wears a shaggy collar of dead fronds
Opened the door on my side and got in.
My father called her Charlotte dear, and said
That I was Susan. Even sitting down,
She was the tallest woman, and she wore
A high fur collar whose white points of hair
Made me want to touch them. They were so soft.
I was excited then, because she helped me
With my present and set me on her lap

So I could see out. We drove a long time,
Through orange groves where all the fruit was green,
Through dairy farms that you could smell right through
The rolled-up windows (Charlotte's perfume smelled
Sweeter though, and so did Daddy's cologne).
We went down through a canyon to the beach
And Charlotte pointed at a black and white
Pair of wings and said it must be a condor.
We saw it drift high up across the canyon.
A roller coaster's highest hump rose up
Against the ocean, where the canyon ended.
Beside it was a dome with scarlet flags.
By this time in the afternoon, at home,
Mother would listen to the radio
And pretty soon I'd have to come indoors
For dinner. Daddy bought me a corn dog,
An Orange Julius, and for dessert,
The biggest cotton candy in the world.
But first I rode the carousel three times.
From there, as I pumped slowly up and down,
I had a good look at the two of them—
Daddy, like a blond boulder, round and bald,
And Charlotte, though I knew how soft she was,
Looking stiff and spiky, like a palm tree.
I knew he loved me (maybe she did, too),
But soon he'd have to take me home to Mother.
A bank of evening fog broke like a wave
Around us, but slowly. It was too cold
To feel soft, too clinging and damp. We left.
Words must have passed between the two of them
After I fell asleep on Charlotte's arm
With her collar pressed lightly on my hair
And Daddy's present open on my lap.
I wish I'd had my say. That single day
Stands out more clearly than my whole childhood.
But I woke next morning in my own bed
And Mother asked if I'd had fun with Daddy.
He'd kidnapped me. She didn't seem to know it!
Daddy never married Charlotte, of course.

And Mother lived as if he were a neighbor
Kindly dropping in to help her with me.
We'll see if that's how I act with your father.
Of all the gifts my own father gave me
I can't remember what was in that box
The day he kidnapped me. That one is lost.

My Mother Really Knew

My father was a tough cookie,
his friends still tell me with a smile.
He was hot-tempered
and had to have his own way,
but they loved him nonetheless,
and so did I.

I remember that
for maybe the first decade of my life
I had to kiss him every night
before I went to bed.

There was one time
he got into a big argument
with the rest of us at dinnertime,
and afterwards when he was in his study
I had to go to sleep
and refused to see him,
a chip off the old block.

But my mother and elder brothers
coaxed me to his door,
and I ran in
and pecked his cheek
without saying a word,
and went to bed
thinking of how unfair life was.

Love, my mother really knew,
was like these islands
formed in part
by tidal waves and hurricanes
and the eruptions of volcanoes,
which suddenly appear
and just as suddenly go away.

Keeping the Horses

The boy had been alone for fifteen days
before the thought occurred to him: this time
maybe the old man wasn't coming back
at all. It was just him and the horses,
feeding their way around the tether-stakes
in a good bit of meadow by the road,
the boy sleeping out with them at night
upon the ground (the nights not yet grown cold),
by daylight watching over them until
he half suspected when he talked to them
they were about to answer—those great eyes,
the telltale shivers in the flank and haunch.
Even the horses had been feeling it,
the small uneasiness that moved inside him.
He brushed them down, went to fetch water
up from the creek a hundred yards away;
hauling it back, he heard the water sway
and lap against the bucket at his side.
A car went by from the farm down the road.
He waved, and the driver waved, and the dust
swept out and made a tunnel in the air—
a tunnel that would suddenly collapse.
And he thought of his mother through the years
trying to glimpse, like that, his father's quick,
authoritative passage through their lives.
He would be drinking now, talking about his plans
with someone he hardly knew in some dark bar,
the truck and van parked outside, the dust
of this same road on top of other dust
from all the roads they'd driven down that year,
following the circuit of the county fairs
with a ramshackle carnival, the horses

sometimes performing in a lot out back
and sometimes to a grandstand audience.
Near towns down those back roads, more and more of late,
they'd pull off onto the grassy shoulder
by a gate that led into a pasture,
backing the animals down the splintered ramp,
his father fashioning a long rope halter
to lead one horse around with at a time
and give the local kids a ride. It cost
two bits some days, on other days a dime,
the difference being what the old man lacked
by way of change to jangle in his jeans.
It always went for drink—always for that.
There was never any money for the boy;
the old man never thought that anyone
had needs except himself. And they were poor,
God, but they were poor! Many a time
they'd lifted out the seat up in the cab,
just to scrounge around for coins: in fun
they called it "going to the bank." (He thought
of the old man, frantic for money now,
lying across the pitted running-board,
his long legs out at angles in the street
like toppled stilts beside the worn-out seat,
hoping to pick up on the littered floor
a beer or two in change . . .)

                         The sun had dipped
into the lower branches of the cottonwoods
down by the creek. Every day now that moment came
a little sooner, and the boy saw how
the grass went deep and almost wet with light
at that lower angle. He walked back down
toward the stand of trees for some kindling wood.
One thing that you could say for the old man:
there was always plenty of food in cans
for cooking over a fire; as for talk,
they'd never come close to running out of that.

Still, with him gone, he didn't miss the talk.
It was good to have the outdoors to himself,
or the feeling of that, the horses there
stirring and nickering, snuffling in the dark
beyond the fire, the stars darting their glints
far back down to him from a wet black sky.
The first few days it seemed to him as if
the old man were still around; but lately
he'd noticed he'd begun to let things go,
begun to grow wild along with the horses.
There were times he wished he could run like them,
the ground reverberating under him,
nothing between him and the open sky
but his shadow floating out over the grass . . .
He rummaged in the canvas knapsack bottom
for the opener. For supper he'd have beans,
cooked in a shallow pan until the bubbles
snapped in the juice like lava on the run—
nothing better, sopped with a hunk of bread.
He thought he'd move the tether-stakes tonight;
then maybe afterwards he'd leave the fire
and walk down by the bridge to listen
to the water gurgling in its glimmering banks.
One of these nights the old man would be back,
and more and more his thoughts were fixed on that.
For several days he'd had a kind of dream
shaping inside his head, a dream in which
he saw himself eyeing his father there
at the firelight's edge—the boy angry
at being left alone to watch the horses,
and running against the old man with his fists.
It was a dream he willed and yet could not
control: always his father in the dream
would catch his wrists and wrap him in his arms,
and the boy, sobbing, had to catch his breath.
It was only a dream—no use to him.
He knew tomorrow, next day, sometime soon,
he'd hear the truck come rattling up the road,

just in time for supper, probably,
the old man getting out and glad to see him,
wiping his mouth on the back of his hand
in that absentminded gesture of his,
as casual as if he had been gone
an hour or two at most, and then he'd say,
"How's my boy?" and ask about the horses.

The Hongo Store, 29 Miles Volcano, Hilo, Hawaii

From a photograph

My parents felt those rumblings
Coming deep from the earth's belly,
Thudding like the bell of the Buddhist Church.
Tremors in the ground swayed the bathinette
Where I lay squalling in soapy water.

My mother carried me around the house,
Back through the orchids, ferns, and plumeria
Of that greenhouse world behind the store,
And jumped between gas pumps into the car.

My father gave it the gun
And said, "Be quiet," as he searched
The frequencies, flipping for the right station
(The radio squealing more loudly than I could cry).

And then even the echoes stopped—
The only sound the Edsel's grinding
And the bark and crackle of radio news
Saying stay home or go to church.

"Dees time she no blow!"
My father said, driving back
Over the red ash covering the road.
"I worried she went go for broke already!"

So in this print the size of a matchbook,
The dark skinny man, shirtless and grinning,
A toothpick in the corner of his smile,
Lifts a naked baby above his head—
Behind him the plate glass of the store only cracked.

My Happiness

That spring day
I stood in the new grass
and watched the man cutting steel
with an arc-welder—
the man my mother had just married.
I watched as he leaned in his welder's mask
and held a blue-white star
to a steel rod until it was glowing with heat.
A cloud drifted in front of the sun
and darkened the land
the way sweat darkened his back.
Then with some slip of the body
or misjudgment of a man
given over wholly to his work
a piece of glowing metal
fell like a tiny meteor into his boot.
His hand went down,
his fingers seared.
Then the smell of burnt flesh,
a groan of pain, and the crazy hopping.
He fumbled in his pocket for a knife,
slit open the boot and swatted the hot metal
off his ankle. What could I do?
I ran for mother and a bucket of water.
And that spring day I remember my happiness
as I poured the cold water over his wound
and she put her arm around his neck
and the sun came out
and the mysterious healing began
and he was saying oh jeezus
and she was saying oh honey.

If Our Dogs Outlived Us

My children learn,
not from the Shih Tzu, Me-Too, who
sits in her dog-nest
on the chaise lounge with the antique needlepoint,
but from Grandma,
what it means to lose a loved one.

Why did Grandma die? asks my youngest,
if Me-Too won't.

Me-Too will die sometime, Darling.

When?

Honey, we've been over this, remember?
A living dog is better than a dead lion?

I set my youngest on my knee
and in unison we say the rest:
For the living know that they shall die:
but the dead know not any thing, neither have they
any more a reward; for the memory
of them is forgotten.

We are lions, Dear One—
our dogs outlive and succeed us
and in so doing, succeed over us.
Like it or not, they're here to stay.
More or less.

Mommy, have you ever seen a dog die?

Yes, Sugar, I have.

What does a dog do when he dies?

My little one is near tears,
so I lighten things up a bit
with an old story Mama told me
when I was young.

Well, he kicks up his heels and says,
Hey, that wasn't so rrrruff!

Is that all?

That's all.
Now down you go.

My little Sheba hops off my lap,
grabs a fistful of horehounds
and runs out back to play.

Mama left all of Grand Granddad's things
to the Shih Tzu who, having shed
over every inch of upholstery,
looks at me with superior eyes.
I'm reminded of the moral
in the old fable, one of Mama's favorites:
Dogs drink at the river Nile running along,
that they may not be seized by the crocodiles.

When I was Sheba's age,
Mama told me the story of Me-Too's name.

Because I want her to follow me, she said.
Only now, do I know what she meant.

Newborn Neurological Exam

no motion and
no sound
but you willing
to breathe

a Q-tip pressed
on open eyes—
nothing

ice water forced
into your ears
nothing

I stand beside you
leash myself to quiet
pray
for pain

Secrets

I doubt that you remember her—except
that final summer when we took the house
beside the bay. I vowed to wait until
right now to tell you how your mother died.
Do you still have her photograph—the one
in which her hands are cupped, with you trying
to peek inside? Every morning even
before I woke, she took you for a walk
to search for starfish scattered on the beach.
You were excited after you returned,
but then you'd sink into a sudden gloom
without a cause that I could see; you'd go
into your room and sit there with your shells,
arranging them in boxes; you'd stay inside
all afternoon. At night your mother talked
about your moods, though in your room, I thought,
when playing with your shells, you seemed content.
You had one smooth quartz stone, your favorite,
and every time we looked you had it placed
inside another box. A thousand times
your mother asked me what I thought that meant.
I thought the stone meant you; the boxes meant
your made-up lives. Your mother thought the stone
was her—that you were putting her away—
but never told you what she guessed. Claiming
they were all beautiful, especially
the rounded stone, you scared us when you said
it was the only one that had itself
inside itself. The way your mouth was fixed
warned us to inquire no more. Your mother
wept all night; we held each other, kissing
gently in the dark, though something private
deep in her sobbing tightened her. She said:
"I don't know why I haven't done things right."

I promised her we'd take a trip, and when
her spirits rose, it seemed to me that you
no longer switched the stone from box to box.
We flew down to Bermuda where we took
a cabin by the beach. At night we strolled
the curving shore, collecting colored stones
and sea-shells to bring home, or curled together,
hugging, naming whatever stars we knew.
She told me things I'd never heard—like once
her mother ran off with her father's friend.
One moonlit evening we undressed each other
on the beach to take a swim. We raced
into the water, holding hands, and then
I let her go so I could watch. Flawless
as polished marble, oh her smooth arms gleamed,
plunging like dolphins as she dove; wind gusts
blew clouds across the moon, and she was gone.
    "Didn't you search for her?" the captain asked,
"Couldn't she swim?" "The water was so dark,"
I said, "and yes, she grew up by the sea."
"Was she depressed?" he asked, and I assured him
she was never happier. "Strange tides,"
I thought I heard him say. Sometimes I dream
that she gets washed up further down the beach,
having forgotten who she is and who
we are, and that she is alive, living
another life. And then I am awake,
wishing something familiar—like the feel
of stone—might bring us back to her. We must
forget the past; we have a new life now.
Alice loves you—she's all you really know
since she moved in with us. Can you recall
your clinging to her on our wedding day,
helping her unpack? You kept the picture
of her sitting on her mother's lap.
    I didn't tell you how your mother died
because so much remained unknown. Promise
never to tell Alice—she's heard enough.
This has to be *our* secret; promise me.
This little golden starfish—take it, Joan—

I've saved it for the necklace that I gave you
when you turned thirteen; your mother bought it
by herself the day before she died.
She said that having secrets was her way
of holding on, and that you'd understand.

Rare Rhythms

All day my father complained
of the noise.
Today they took it down,
that massive elm across the street
(unproclaimed family crest),
cut down and carted away
in a yellow truck.
On the lawn below these turret windows,
hands in his sweater pockets,
he is walking over to inspect
the job. Still with his morning moodiness,
his gait is unusually stiff
but he bends from the waist like a boy,
draws a hand in circles
over the fresh cross-section,
thinking of the years,
a hundred, easily, spent,
in perfect spangles of wood,
rimmed reminders
of old nests.

I see him stop with the stump behind him
and for a moment I worry
he'll sit down on it and look ridiculous
and old. This morning when he snapped
over breakfast I knew it wasn't
only the noise—the gnarling argument
of the saw drowning out the birds,
the scrape of silver against our plates—
but my departure,
my visit too short again.

Now he looks up, sees me in the turret,
waves and heads back over,
the longish graying hair he combs straight
back lifted comically by the wind.

They're new, these things he takes time for—
fills the feeders in the yard,
watches the cat. He'll even climb
the two flights to watch the sun go down
from this empty room. He rarely came up
when I lived here,
where we slept—my boyfriend and I,
teenagers anxiously testing his reticence.
But one night, one midnight, he did come up
and stood with his back to the jamb
to tell us, too quietly,
that he had come from frantic hours
in a police holding room with a woman,
a patient of his
who had driven her daughter out after dinner,
shot and killed her
behind the synagogue.
He lingered a long time in the room
absently scanning my strewn clothes
and sheet music, answering our questions,
talking slowly about the confusion, the husband,
the other children at the house,
his patient he couldn't calm.
And all because the daughter
was moving to Boston
where her lover,
a black man, was waiting.
And before he went down,
his eyes red with exhaustion,
he kissed us, both,
almost absentmindedly.

I hear that rare rhythm
of his hard shoes on the stairs—
familiar stranger that he is
to this room—he won't notice
the huge gap in the foliage
beyond these windows, he'll ask
what he can carry down.

Dreamers and Flyers

1.

The day my father and Jack Grimes,
Confident as angels, in love with space,
Took off their toy-sized monoplane
Into the test of heaven,
I shut my eyes so tight, they stung.
Then everyone was cheering—even mother,
Transfixed by a dreamer's crazy faith again.
Anything I build, I fly, he said.
And fly, it did,
Absurdly small against that waste of blue,
But elegant as a dragonfly,
It larked and lazed upon the clear airstream
In a child's dream of flying.

A child's dream of flying?
Maybe it was the distances between
One lonely Kansas farm and another farm
Or the distances he measured staring up
Into the sky's depths
That raced his thoughts like manic Ferris wheels
To flying, flying, flying—
And swept him to this easy landing
In a baked and stubbled Kansas field.
She flies like a dream, he said, and grinned
At my proffered sunflower.

2.

Now his portrait hangs in the opulent anteroom
Of a great company, whose dreamers launch
Leviathans that streak the sky
With a thousand contrails,
And stitch the continents like country quilts.

His portrait, there, among five others—
Barnstormers, all—or boys who tinkered T's
In scorched Midwestern sheds
And never lost that purity of fooling.

I think of him then
Spread-eagled on his back to study clouds,
The small clouds in their sleepy flocks
That tamed the Kansas sky—
The motes that swam like gold dust in his eye
When he watched the hawk stall
With perfect concentration in mid-flight
And then resume its sunward arc.

Could there have been
A brilliant aerial circus in his head,
Racket of wings, of tiny furious motors
That whined above the buzzing in his ears
From fiddlers in the clover,
And haunted him to make the dreaming real?

I like to think he would approve
My larking about with words, my taking wing
In a child's dream of flying—
                    That there's blood likeness in it.

Grape Sherbet

The day? Memorial.
After the grill
Dad appears with his masterpiece—
swirled snow, gelled light.
We cheer. The recipe's
a secret and he fights
a smile, his cap turned up
so the bib resembles a duck.

That morning we galloped
through the grassed-over mounds
and named each stone
for a lost milk tooth. Each dollop
of sherbet, later,
is a miracle,
like salt on a melon that makes it sweeter.

Everyone agrees—it's wonderful!
It's just how we imagined lavender
would taste. The diabetic grandmother
stares from the porch,
a torch
of pure refusal.

We thought no one was lying
there under our feet,
we thought it
was a joke. I've been trying
to remember the taste,
but it doesn't exist.
Now I see why
you bothered,
father.

Child in a Blue Linen Dress

Too aware of endings, I search among
blue flowers of long ago summers
to find first things, something to comfort
my questioning spirit, and find myself,
small and happy, in a blue linen dress,
admiring my Roman sandals, their patent leather
straps circling my legs, holding in place
the silk knee socks, hiding scars of chigger bites.

I was six years old then; a boy cousin,
handsome at eight, had kissed me behind
my grandmother's cedars; I had run to hide my face
in my mother's skirts, making her taffeta
petticoat rustle. It was a family reunion.
Children ate at the "second table"
—chicken wings and gizzards. It was all done out
of doors, the long table spread under maple trees.

Just before the passing of eggs purple with beet juice
a worm dropped out of a tree onto my mother's neck.
She fainted dead away and became the life of the party.
And I was proud because she was my mother
and I had on my blue linen dress.

My Mother and the Touched
Old Woman

When my mother fell from the cherry tree
because of the bites driving her neighbor crazy,
she wrenched just about everything and ended up
flat on her back in St. Joe's, the first time ever
she had to sleep on sheets for the crippled
—but that's not the whole ball of wax.
In the next bed was a touched old woman.
How did my mother know this? Listen.
                                        The old woman
didn't trust her son and daughter-in-law any more,
they wanted to turn her out from the house where she raised
five babies and watered God's sweetest peppers by the back stoop.
They said at her age she couldn't digest them so why bother?
My mother at this point felt for the old woman—
didn't *she* grow peppers too and sometimes sit right
down on the ground and eat one straight from the stalk
all beaded up with little pops of dew in the morning?
How could that son turn his own mother out?
                                        So
when they were coming to visit my mother was firmly
prepared to defend this poor old woman who was tiny
like her own mother only nowhere near as strong because just
for starters she never milked ten cows every morning come
hell or high water and then plucked a chicken for lunch—who can
eat soup without stock?—but that's another story. Suddenly
the woman raised up, half dead, and told about a suitcase
hidden under the bed—and would my mother please
do her a favor? Well, how can you say no despite the pinch
in your neck and the handsome specialist they'd had to call off
his fancy country club two days earlier when Joy poor thing
quit holding the ladder to get at those ankles being
eaten alive by mosquitoes, saying don't move

anything or else. And naturally he scared her.
                                                    But
despite all that my mother crawled out of bed, got the
suitcase on pins and needles and hauled it
to the closet the old woman's shaky finger pointed at.
"Up on top! Up on top!" she squawked at my mother
and so my mother dragged over a chair and climbed up how
she'll never know and that's when the touched part came in
—with my mother standing stiff as a board trying to
push the suitcase farther back on the shelf and not
twist her neck and catch hell from the doctor for throwing
half her body and it's anybody's guess what else out of kilter
and the old woman yelling bloody murder like my mother's friend
Angie did one time at the mouse she found on the angel-
food cake, that she cashed in everything, all her
bonds and stocks and something in a sock and every last
penny was *there*, in one lump, fifty thousand smackers!
                                                    Well,
you guessed it, my mother said. In *he* struts
all suntanned, white teeth, a little red pony rearing up
on his pretty shirt, but swearing a blue streak, you'd think
in medical school they'd learn to smile back
at a lady, and then she thought fifty thousand dollars, what if
they come in now, the cold fish, and accuse her of
trying to steal that old woman's money! She never stole
anything unless you counted stingy Solack's apples the next
farm over and that was, well it was years ago, snot-nosed
kids having fun and who counts wormy apples? Which was
what she had here if you get her drift.
                                        In a split second
my mother knew what to do. No doctor no matter
how handsome he was was going to swear her
back to a cold bed beside a rich old touched woman who
now was squawking about a silver rooster you tipped over
to pour salt from its tail and how she loved it and no more
of God's green peppers in the same breath—
she could eat noodles and butter, they were just as good.
Besides, she got this far, she could go
the rest of the way herself.

The Storyteller

I'll tell you what is real,
but not all at once. A long
list, a dry one. I get parched
sometimes, have to speak with
my eyes. With them, I can tell
things loud enough for a nearly
blind man to hear, if he tries.

> Part of what I know is this,
> that summer thunder rumbles
> in a clear sky just to tease
> the man who can't believe
> what he doesn't see. Rain
> grows cloud crops by rising
> straight up from hot ground.

With my hands I can carve
stories, make them live, run
on long legs from my mind
into yours. And what I know

> is this, every bird with wings
> flies, even if only in its soul.
> They are all birds, after all.

Other times, I run past dry,
my eyes hurt from brightness,
and my hands lie flat, still.
Then you have to touch me
to hear, to know what's real.

The Last Mountain Lion on Maple Crest Mountain

As told in the barbershop

Out there where Barnum Road hooks left
and disappears in the scrub
I was just out for turkey
doing my turkey call CHIK CHIK CHIK
worrying about all the rain
and how my potatoes was drowning like pups—
and there he was, not yellow
like you see on the goddamn television
but graylike, slick as a button
and looking at me, hard. No,
no way he was just some overgrown bobcat,
that sucker was big as that table of yours
with a tail this long. Why ain't you heard
this before? Because nobody
never told nobody nothing, that's why.
I weren't drinking, neither, don't even
like the smell since I gave the stuff up
when me and Bob Willis shot
Pop Korsky's truck two years ago.
I been living here twenty years
and ain't never seen even an otter before
and Bob Willis has caught three, can you believe
that bastard, but it's been worth the wait—
I think someone wanted me to see that sonofabitch
before they drag my old bones away
and that's God's own unvarnished truth.

Johnny Spain's White Heifer

The first time ever I saw Johnny Spain was
the first day I came to this town. There
he was, lantern jaw and broken nose, wall-eyed and
fractious, with a can of beer in one hand and a
walkie-talkie in the other, out in front
of the post office. And I heard someone saying,
"Johnny, what in hell are you doing?" "I'm looking,"
he answered, in an executive tone, "for me goddamn
white heifer." "Run off, did she?" "Yass,"
he said. "Busted me south-side fence, the bitch—
if some thieving bastard didn't bust it for her."
"You reckon she's running loose on Main Street?"
Johnny looked down, then up, then sideways, or possibly
all three together. "Hell, no," he growled.
"She's off there somewheres." He swung his beer can
in a circle. "Me boys is up in the hills, looking.
I'm di-recting the search." Then he turned away
to a crackle on the walkie-talkie.
                                    And that
was how Johnny liked it. He wasn't much
on farming, although his farm could have been
a fine one—closest to town, up on the hillside
overlooking the feed mill. But Johnny's curse
was a taste for administration. The "farm" was no more
than a falling-down barn, some mixed head
of cattle, and a flock of muddy ducks. Johnny
was the first man in the volunteer fire department
to have one of those revolving blue lights
set up on top of his car, and Johnny Spain
was *always* going to a fire. When he came down
off that hill of his in that air-borne '65 Pontiac—
look out! It was every man for himself
when Johnny was on the highway.

                                   I used to think
sometimes I had a glimpse of that white heifer
that Johnny never found. "A goddamn beauty,"
he'd say. "By Jesus, she was. Why, I give
five whole greenback dollars cash and a pair
of Indian runners to Blueball Baxter for her
when she were a calf—there wan't a finer heifer
in the whole goddamn county." I'd see a flash
of white in the balsams at the upper end of the pasture
or in the thickets across the brook when I looked up
at twilight; but I never found her. Probably
all I saw was a deer-tail flashing.
                                   After
they changed the town dump into a sanitary
land fill operation the selectmen hired Johnny
for custodian, and they gave him a little Michigan
dozer to bury the trash with. Johnny loved it.
"Dump it over there," he'd holler. "Goddamn it,
can't you see the sign? Tires and metal
go on the other side." One time he even
inaugurated a system of identification cards,
so people from Centerville and Irishtown
would quit using our dump, and by God
you had to show your pass, even if Johnny
had known you for years. Part of the deal
was salvage, of course. Johnny could take
whatever he wanted from the accumulated junk
and sell it. Trouble was he mostly didn't
or couldn't sell it, so it wound up in his
barnyard, everything from busted baby carriages
to stacks of old lard kegs from the diner,
up there to be viewed by whoever cared to look.
And the one with the best view was Mel Barstow,
son of the mill owner, who lived on the hill
above the other side of town. There they were,
two barons above the burg, facing each other
at opposite ends, like the West Wind and the East Wind
on an old-time map. Mel had everything

he thought he wanted—a house like a two-page spread
in *House and Garden*, for instance, and a wife
that was anyone's envy, and a pair of binoculars
with which he liked to watch the gulls flying
over the river. Of course he'd seen Johnny's place
many a time, but one evening he focused down
on that barnyard, then quick got on the phone.
"Johnny, why in hell don't you clean up that mess
over there? It's awful. It's a disgrace." Johnny
didn't say much. But a couple of nights later,
maybe an hour past dark, he phoned up Mel.
"Mel," he said, "I got me a pair of them by-
nockyewlars over to Morrisville this forenoon,
and I been a-studying them goddamn birds out there,
and what I want to know is why in the hell
you don't tell that good-looking female of yours
to put some clothes on her backside when she's parading
up and down behind that picture window? Picture, hell—
I'll say it's a picture! It's a goddamn frigging
dis-grace, if you want to know the truth."
                                        Well,
I expect for a while Mel's wife was the one
that would have liked to get lost, and maybe
Mel too, because it's a cinch you can't go down
to buy even a pack of Winstons at the IGA
without running into Johnny Spain, and of course
Johnny's the one that knows exactly, exactly
how to keep the sting alive, winking wall-eyed
both ways at once, grinning that three-toothed grin.

But Johnny Spain's white heifer was what was lost.
She wasn't found. Wherever she is, she's gone.
Oh, I'm not the only one who thought they saw her,
because reports kept coming in, all the way round
from the Old Settlement clear up to Mariveau's
gravel pit. But that's all they were, just
reports. She'd have made a first-rate cow,
I reckon, if a man could have caught her, only
of course somewhat more than a mite wild.

Why Rosalie Did It

Because talk in the town
had the galvanized taste
of tapwater standing
too long in pipes

because dogs ran loose
sniffing each other's rearends
while people walked
their personal devils on a leash
or carried them, like cobras
in a laundry basket

because all the talk
the telling and recollecting
enlarged, clarified nothing
but wore memory away
so when Mrs. Curry was killed
crossing the road to her mailbox
she became no more
than a dead dog on the interstate
run over and over (in the telling)
until nothing was left but
a scrap of hair in a bloody spot

because they refused to interpret
("that's just his way"
("well, he was a Meadors"
("them Jacksons is like that")

because the 40-watt bulbs
at the head of stairs
were one with their little economies
of word, of thought

because, stopped on the street
in front of the hardware store, talking,
they were like horses standing
side by side, head to tail,
swishing flies off one another

because they knew
everything
about everybody

knew when her Daddy died
choked on a piece of beef
at Purcell's Family Restaurant
after church
he had a polaroid of Roma Strickland, naked,
in his wallet

because they knew
or thought they knew
everything
about everybody

because you were naked here anyway
Rosalie came up from under the bridge
at the end of the town
—her jeans and shirt and underwear already
floating downriver—and
ran buck naked down Main
at 4:30 in the afternoon
blonde hair flying
tan all over
(they didn't know that, for instance)
no white skin where she'd worn
any two-piece bathing suit

because at least for the two minutes
it took to jog past the Dollar General,
past Western Auto, All Star
Realty and Auction, and on out

to where she'd parked her Datsun
by the picnic tables
the boys from the Job Corps built

nobody moved
nobody spoke

nobody knew what to think or say
There wasn't a sound
except her bare feet touching lightly
on the astonished sidewalk
nothing moved
except her reflection running with her
in store windows.

Oliver Johnson Comes Back to Bed the Morning after the Ice Storm and Tells His Wife Why

No sooner had I drunk
my morning coffee
and stepped out the back
than I saw three pheasants,
down the lane,
filling their crops
with jewels
and all around
the stubble-fields sparkling.
It was something.
And then the horses
came out of the barn,
steaming in the cold,
and licked,
as lazy as you please,
the ice off the fence posts.
I just stood there
with my workgloves in my hands.
Who could do chores
on a morning like this?
Not me, God knows.
Even the lilac was borne down
by the diamonds on its back.

A Kinsman

All those years
my great-grandfather stood in his oval frame,
his hand on the back of a chair—
black beard, black hat, black Sunday coat—
looking as if he knew something I didn't.
All those years.
I never suspected
he really was hiding something.

Nor did my mother.
But cleaning the frame one day,
she took him out and found, behind him,
a second picture, an old tintype,
a cloudy face, little more than a shadow.

At first we said the two men favored.
Then we couldn't be sure.
We searched our memories, the scanty records.
We carried the tintype to great-aunts,
brought it out when distant cousins came.
Nobody knew him.

Maybe because he seemed to belong there,
we put him back in the frame
behind the glint in my great-grandfather's eye.

I think of him there, pressed
like a leaf between pages of a book.
And then of those lives, nameless to us,
and numerous as summer leaves, who flourished,
withered and fell, gathered
to the ground like leaves that drifted down
fall mornings when their breath came in clouds.

I think of him there in the dark,
his image a melting cloud, a shadow.
I claim him as a kinsman, a life
behind our lives. I move closer
and cloud the oval frame's glass with my breath.

The Emeritus

". . . Love, in his imperishable youth,
is, I repeat, the youngest of them all."

The Symposium

If ever there were a time for her
to come back with a saving message
it was now—the whole world on fire
with spring sun and he too old
to escape, and the young, oblivious,
swimming in lazy shoals, half-
naked across his thick lenses
to and from afternoon class
past the bench he sat on, Plato
open on his lap, the page
so unreadably brilliant, his eyes
turned to water, so he shut them,
not to seem crying, an old fool
gone soft in the sensorium,
weak in the vision; but still the light
burned through as a sullen
red glow or haze, and it was
against this infernal background
that he saw her—and just as she was
forty years back, alone
on that remote beach.
              Only now,
she cradled an armful of yellow iris
and was turned as though attending someone
in the dark beside her—but the same brown hair
unloosened, tumbling in a dense tangle
of shiny coils to her long waist,
the same wide, woundable mouth,

slightly crooked, so it seemed
a permanently sad half smile,
the same gray eyes, cloudier now,
seen through so many layers of death,
and the same secretness that all else
about her only hinted at,
the very thing he loved most and knew
from the first would be the dear subject
of his great study from then on,
as he watched her gathering shells,
or mosses under redwoods, or sitting
with sewing on her lap, watched
with the concentration of a man
set for signs, or listened hard
to her voice—tentative and soft
as though spoken across the low rush
of water—not for what she said,
but for the something hidden just
inside her saying it. Or right
in the middle of class, he lecturing
on some tragedy—rows
of upturned, bored, and courteous
young faces waiting—he'd stop,
wanting to be alone with the thought
of her, as with an urgent mystery
to be explained: how this beauty or wholeness
could seem to come from something like pain,
or could be made up from odd things
that shouldn't fit together but did
(brown hair, gray eyes, the crooked smile),
or why her secretness had chosen
him as its keeper, the one other
in the world who might just understand,
or, failing that, protect and cherish it
if it took a whole lifetime of watching,
which was a kind of joy he felt
could go on forever—but that was a fable,
as he learned in his own classroom

on a day much like any other,
when they entered, pale, led him out
into the hall and revealed the truth:
her heart failed her. He didn't know
about her heart.
                    What followed
was an interminable ceremony
of shadows, trailing in
and out by cemetery paths
among dark clouds of comforters,
concluding in the solitude
of his small study, the spines of his books
glowing with dusty autumn sun
and he, fevered, seeming to doze
into the only dream he could still
wholly remember: the white city
on a slope pasturing gently down
to a blue bay, a few sails
gleaming in the sunrise. He
and a choice friend (no one he knew
outside the dream) stood together
softly conversing before a small
and spotless temple when the friend
pointed to a girl in peplum
running in easy strides along
the shore below, almost transparent
in waterflash and hard sunlight,
and he said simply, as though this
were the long-sought answer, "A nymph,"
and woke crying with glad relief,
but recalled what he'd lost in the waking
and renounced all dreams, swore never
again to be taken in by the romance
of nearness, never again to believe
more than there is, and to serve out
his appointed term with the withered self
left behind when the mourners departed,
and swore also, after a second

full tumbler of brandy, to burn
his books, but instead stumbled out
blind into the pitching darkness,
through the campus gates and into his own
vacant room where he scrawled brutally
on the moonlit blackboard, "What
you know, you know," over and over,
as though this were assigned for a lesson
unlearned, and woke up under his desk,
aching in the cold pallor of dawn,
amazed at the poverty of truth,
or, forty years later, having now
served out his appointed term—
woke up here where he could sit
on sunny days like an old lizard
on a stone, measuring the distance
between one sort of ignorance
and another, knowing what
he knew.
        But today was different,
a day of first or last things,
of messages from beyond belief,
a day of fire, the library
ablaze, the new science building
and the old brick barn where they stored
the humanities, and the young themselves,
each fringed with a soft flame
like an aura, and the book in his lap burning,
and the fire piercing the skin of his eyelids,
before whose glow she still stood,
more like a daughter than a wife,
and it was now she turned to him
with that smile and he hated it, as though,
after his sucking the salty stone
of renunciation all these years,
she was calling him out to some vague,
second-rate version of love, fit
only for an old idiot supposed

only to ask her blessing now,
beg her to sit with him and rejoice
in this final desolation of light,
all-forgiving fellow inmates
of time, God's spies, singing
and making jokes about who's in,
and who's out—No! That's the cruelest
of all fables and he dismissed her,
opening his eyes on what was merely
there, though all he saw at first
were dark after-images
that stung his vision, and then the young—
still burning and oblivious,
and some who passed close, smiling at him,
so it was only then he discovered
he'd been smiling himself for some time,
not at them (let them think
as they please), but at her, her,
incredulous that finally she meant
simply he was alive, if mostly
to pain, which, of course, explained
nothing. The armful of iris then
was a gift, not given to keep,
but maybe acknowledge by granting its beauty,
granting it and giving it up,
and also maybe giving up
the little fossil self he thought
he'd preserved against pain and joy alike,
giving it up for what he knew not,
maybe another kind of dream
maybe nothing, but maybe . . .
                                    And so,
closing his book, he whispered
to her absence: "I'll be wiser
hereafter," meaning many
contradictory things, and beside him
on the bench, the young man with beard
and guitar turned with random attention

to ask in a voice sweet with tolerance,
"What?" And it was just at that question
the campanile bells began
to sound the latest hour, high
archaic commemoration of what
had passed and what was yet to come,
and the old man, stuck forever
in the present, answered the young one,
not unkindly, "Nothing, nothing."

Martha Nelson Speaks

COLUMBUS, OHIO, Sept. 24 (UPI)—On June 25, 1876,
Gen. George Custer made his last stand at the battle of the
Little Big Horn. Also on that day, Martha Nelson completed
her first year in a mental institution. She is still there. Miss
Nelson, who was 102 last June, has spent the last 97 years at
Orient State Institute near here, formerly the Columbus
State Institute for the Feeble-minded. She was committed in
1875. But her records were destroyed in a fire in 1883 and no
one knows for sure why she is at the institute. "She has
never had a chance," said Dr. A. Z. Soforenko, superinten-
dent of the institution. "It is a wasted life. She is quite co-
herent for her age. She has no relatives and has had no con-
tact with anybody for the last 78 to 80 years."

The New York Times, September 25, 1973.

I came into oxygen
102 years ago
with my vast little body intact
and all my selves unlayering,
but my mother wept
and my father scowled
because I was one too many.
And when in time
I began to talk
my brothers and sisters sneered,
so all my speech
was with myself
and my secret family and friends.
Yet I had much to say
and much to observe in my own way.
But when they watched my lips,
many times moving silently,
with nods and shaking head and smiles,
they put me down as simple
and left me here at Columbus State.

My parents would come
just once a year
and say a few words,
but not darling or dear,
and I said no words that they could hear.
At seventeen I saw the last of them
and never knew when they died.
I have no photographs of me at home
nor any of me at the Institute,
so I only know myself as I am.
I do have acquaintance in the place
but since they're all deficient
I rely on those within.
I learned to read in the early days
and have talked to the staff for a century
but have never heard the truth of my life.
I gave up mourning long ago
for the husband, children, friends I missed,
but often in the mirror
I scan my ancient face
and say, "Martha, little Martha,
was it written before you were born
that in a hundred years or so
you would be marooned on an empty planet
in loveless space?"

A Grandfather's Last Letter

Elise, I have your valentine with the red shoes, I have
Waited too many weeks to write—wanting to describe
The excitement on the back lawn for you:
                              the forsythia

Is now a bright yellow, and with the ribbons you draped
Inside it, trembles in a breeze,
All yellows and blues, like that pilot light this winter
Worried by just a little breath that came out of you.

On the dark side of the barn there's the usual railing
Of snow.
The tawny owl, nightingales, and moles
Have returned to the lawn again.

I have closed your grandmother's front rooms.

I know you miss her too. Her crocus bed showed its first
Green nose this morning. For breakfast I had
A duck's egg and muffins.

Your father thinks I shouldn't be alone?
Tell him I have planted a row of volunteer radishes.
I have replaced the north window . . .

So you have read your first book. Sewed a dress for
The doll. The very young and old are best at finding
Little things to do. The world is jealous of us, you know?

The moles are busy too. Much more mature this year,
The boar with the black velvet coat made a twelve
Foot long gallery under the linden where the mockingbirds
Are nesting.

The moles took some of my rags to add to
Their nursery of grass, leaves, and roots.
The cream-colored sow is yet to make her appearance!
They have seven mounds. Each with three bolt doors
Or holes.
The pine martens are down from the woods, I see them
In the moonlight waiting for a kill.

Molehills can weaken a field so that a train
Passing through it sinks suddenly, the sleepers
In their berths sinking too!

I wonder what it's like in their underground rooms:
Their whiskers telegraphing the movements
Of earthworms. They don't require water when on
A steady diet of nightcrawlers. Worms are almost
Entirely made of water.

Last night there was quite an incident. The sun was going
Down and the silly boar was tunneling toward
The linden and he went shallow, the owl dropped down
Setting its claws into the lawn, actually taking hold
Of the blind mole, at that moment the mockingbird,
Thinking her nest threatened, fell on the owl putting
Her tiny talons into his shoulders. Well,

There they were, Elise, the owl on top of the invisible
Mole, the mockingbird on top of the owl. The mole
Moved backwards a foot,
The birds were helpless and moved with him.
They formed quite a totem. The two birds looked so serious
In their predicament. A wind brushed the wash on the line.
And our three friends broke each for its respective zone.

Tomorrow the vines on the house are coming down. 1 want
The warmth of the sun on that wall. I'm sending
You a package with some of your grandmother's old clay
Dolls, silverware, and doilies.

Tell your father he is not coming in June to kill
The moles! Tell him to go fishing instead, or to take
Your mother to Florida.

You said you worry that someday I'll be dead also! Well,
Elise, of course, I will. I'll be hiding then from your world
Like our moles. They move through their tunnels
With a swimming motion. They don't know where they're going—

But they go.

There's more to this life than we know. If ever
You're sleeping in a train on the northern prairies
And everything sinks a little
But keeps on going, then, you've visited me in another world—

Where I am going.

When Angels Came to Zimmer

One morning a great gaggle slid
Down through holes in clouds,
Twirling like maple seeds
Through trees to the windowscreen.
Fervent as new tussock moths,
They flapped and dashed themselves,
Smearing their heavenly dust,
Until Zimmer, in pity and alarm,
Opened to let them into his study.
They flew in with smiles and sighs,
Making him bashful, as if a dozen
Gorgeous chorus girls had suddenly
Pranced into the room.
                          They perched on
Bookshelves, cigar stubs and beer cans;
One even tried to sit on Zimmer's lap.
All day they danced the Lindy,
And some, not knowing better, dabbled
Their darling toes in the toilet bowl.
They sang chorus after chorus of
"Stardust" and "Moonlight in Vermont,"
Constantly touching and stroking Zimmer.
Then at day's end, as if someone
Had rung a bell, they stood to sing
A final chorus of "Deep Purple."
With a whoosh of air and expensive perfume,
They fluttered from the room and ascended.
Zimmer stepped out to watch them rise
And flapped his dirty hankie at the stars.

ACKNOWLEDGMENTS

Permission to reprint poems is gratefully acknowledged to the following:

Mike Angelotti for "The Last Man Killed by Indians in Kimble County, Texas" and "Still Life."

Atheneum Publishers, an imprint of Macmillan Publishing Company, for "Tending the Garden" from *For the New Year* by Eric Pankey, copyright © 1984 by Eric Pankey.

Mary Baron for "Newborn Neurological Exam."

George Bogin for "Cottontail" (first appeared in *New Letters*), copyright © 1985 by George Bogin; "The Kiss" (first appeared in *Confrontation*), copyright © 1986 by George Bogin; and "Martha Nelson Speaks," copyright © 1986 by George Bogin.

Christopher Buckley for "White" from *Other Lives* (Ithaca House, 1985).

Carnegie-Mellon University Press for "Grape Sherbert" from *Museum* by Rita Dove; and "In the Spring" and "What Saundra Said About Being Short" from *False Statements* (Carnegie-Mellon University Press, 1986) by Jim Hall.

Hayden Carruth and Sheepmeadow Press for "Johnny Spain's White Heifer," copyright © 1978 by Hayden Carruth.

Jared Carter for "The Madhouse" (originally appeared in *Indianapolis Journal*), copyright © 1976, 1981 by Jared Carter; "The Purpose of Poetry" (originally appeared in *Images*), copyright ©

Garrett Hongo for "The Hongo Store, 29 Miles Volcano, Hilo, Hawaii."

Houghton Mifflin Company for "Around the Campfire" and "Postcards of the Hanging: 1869" from *After the Lost War* by Andrew Hudgins, copyright © 1988 by Andrew Hudgins; and "At the Piano" from *Saints and Strangers* by Andrew Hudgins, copyright © 1985 by Andrew Hudgins.

Mark Jarman for "The Gift."

David Jauss for "The Ghost Dance: August, 1976" (originally appeared in *Waters: Journal of the Arts*); and "Oliver Johnson Comes Back to Bed . . ." (originally appeared in *Poetry Now*).

Alfred A. Knopf, Inc. for "Maud" from *Driving the Body Back* by Mary Swander, copyright © 1985, 1986 by Mary Swander.

Joan LaBombard for "Dreamers and Flyers" (first appeared in *The California Quarterly*, Summer 1971).

Sara London for "Rare Rhythms" (first appeared in the *Carolina Quarterly*, Winter 1985), copyright © 1985 by Sara London.

Longhouse (Green River, Brattleboro, Vt.) for "The Dog Poisoner" by Keith Wilson, copyright © 1984 by Keith Wilson.

Louisiana State University Press for "Early Love" from *Durations* by Herbert Scott, copyright © 1987 by Herbert Scott.

Wing Tek Lum for "My Mother Really Knew" from *Expounding the Doubtful Points* (Honolulu, 1987).

George Ella Lyon for "The Courtship" (first appeared in *Poet and Critic*, Vol. 14, no. 1); and "Progress" (first appeared in *Appalachian Journal*, Vol. 11, nos. 1–2/Autumn-Winter 1983–84).

Helen Sorrells for "Child in a Blue Linen Dress."

Frank Steele for "Close to Home" and "Moving" (originally appeared in *The Literary Review*, 1969).

University of Georgia Press for "Celestial" from *American Light* by Michael Pettit, copyright © 1984 by the University of Georgia Press.

University of Iowa Press for "Driving Lesson" from *Cardinal Points* by Michael Pettit, copyright © 1988 by the University of Iowa Press.

University of Pittsburgh Press for "The Last Mountain Lion on Maple Crest Mountain" from *Night Watch on the Chesapeake* by Peter Meinke, copyright © 1987 by Peter Meinke; "My Happiness" from *Border Crossings* by Greg Pape, copyright © 1978 by Greg Pape; "Cruel Boys," "Finding a Lucky Number," and "Oranges" from *Black Hair* by Gary Soto, copyright © 1985 by Gary Soto; "Constipation" from *People and Dog in the Sun* by Ronald Wallace, copyright © 1987 by Ronald Wallace; and "Lester Tells of Wanda and the Big Snow" and "When Angels Came to Zimmer" from *Family Reunion* by Paul Zimmer, copyright © 1983 by Paul Zimmer.

Viking Penguin Inc. for "The Flood" from *The Descent* by Ann Stanford, copyright © 1969 by Ann Stanford.

Don Welch for "The Chicken Poem" from *The Rarer Game* (Kearney State College Press, 1980).

Wesleyan University Press for "Ophelia" from *White Dress* by Brenda Hillman, copyright © 1985.

Edward E. Wilson for "Autumnal Equinox."

Gary Young for "To Raise a Chimney" (originally appeared in *The Ontario Review*).

Ree Young for "The Storyteller."